WHEN HELPING YOU IS HURTING ME

WHEN HELPING YOU IS HURTING ME

Escaping the Messiah Trap

Carmen Renee Berry

1817

Harper & Row, Publishers, San Francisco

Cambridge, Hagerstown, New York, Philadelphia, Washington
London, Mexico City, São Paulo, Singapore, Sydney

WHEN HELPING YOU IS HURTING ME. Copyright © 1988 by Carmen Renee Berry. All rights reserved. Printed in the United States of America. No part of this book may be used or reproduced in any manner whatsoever without written permission except in the case of brief quotations embodied in critical articles and reviews. For information address Harper & Row, Publishers, Inc., 10 East 53rd Street, New York, NY 10022. Published simultaneously in Canada by Fitzhenry and Whiteside, Limited, Toronto.

FIRST HARPER & ROW PAPERBACK EDITION PUBLISHED IN 1989

Library of Congress Cataloging-in-Publication Data

Berry, Carmen Renee.
  When helping you is hurting me.

  Bibliography: p.
  Includes index.
  1. Self-sacrifice.   2. Child psychology.
3. Self-sacrifice—Case studies.   I. Title.
II. Title: Messiah trap.
BF637.S42B47   1988   158'.2   87-45685
ISBN 0-06-060788-2
ISBN 0-06-250050-3 (pbk.)

90   91   92   93   94   FAIR   10   9   8   7   6   5   4   3   2   1

For my mother and father

And for the "good kids" who have fallen into
the Messiah Trap

Contents

Preface

This book was conceived through the combination of my professional observation and personal journey. As a therapist, I began working primarily with child and adult victims of child sexual abuse. The more I worked with victims of abuse and the more committed I became to combatting child abuse on a larger scale, the more convinced I became that efforts must be made in the area of prevention. To prevent child molestation, I reasoned, we must better understand people who perpetrate this crime. Consequently, in the early 1980s, I began to interview men convicted of child molestation.

I entered those barred rooms with the expectation of meeting up with "monsters"—vile and almost nonhuman beings for whom I would feel hatred and repulsion. It was impossible for me to fathom how I could have anything in common with someone who had sexually violated a child. I was surprised by the many "normal" faces that greeted me—faces of sadness, confusion, rage.

Ten of these men volunteered to be interviewed on audiotape, to help educate parents and others on how to protect children from molestation. Two outstanding features from those interviews eventually became the basis for *When Helping You Is Hurting Me.*

The first came as a result of answering my question "How did you choose a child to molest?" The answer was consistent: "I chose a kid who reminded me of myself when I was a child—vulnerable, lonely, innocent." As we explored further, each man described how he was molested or physically violated as a young boy. Unable and unwilling to address their own victimization in a direct manner, however, these offenders vicariously experienced the pain, rage, horror, and sadness of their victims.

My discussions with these sex offenders began to resemble my sessions with those clients in my practice who were victims of abuse. Similarities emerged as well as contrasts between the two populations, with a consistent overlap—both victims and offenders had experienced violation as children. I realized that offenders were human after all: in fact, they were very much like the hurt little children in my client load.

The second insight hit much closer to home as I realized that these ten sex offenders and I did have something in common—victims. We both seemed to need to have a relationship with someone in pain.

When I asked, "Why do you continue to molest children when you know it is harmful?" The offenders' answers held the same despair and helplessness that might be felt by the alcoholic or drug addict: "I hate myself when I do it and I want to stop, but I don't know how." These men seemed driven, addicted, to having intense, emotional, yet hurtful relationships with their victims.

As I observed my own behavior and those of many mental health professionals with whom I worked, I saw a similar compulsion. We also seemed driven, even addicted, to having intense and emotional relationships—only *we* were trying to *help*. As I drove away from the prison that day, I was hounded by questions that filled my mind: "Why do I spend all my time helping others? Could I stop if I tried, or am I addicted to helping? Why did I choose to work with people in pain? Could it be because, like the offender, I am not willing to face my own pain directly?"

I took an honest look at my life and what I saw surprised me. I thought I was doing the "right" thing by helping people. But by helping others, I avoided being intimate with them. I set myself up as a better, more "together" person. The truth is, I was hurting, deeply hurting, but I didn't know how to signal for help.

I began to communicate more honestly with my friends and colleagues about the pain and various concerns in my life. They responded by sharing more openly about their inner selves. It was difficult for us to move from behind the protection of our professional roles and to acknowledge our mutual vulnerabilities. We were much more comfortable helping than we were asking for help. I found that, while many professional and lay persons perform their helping duties in a balanced manner, many of us are addicted to helping. We have to help because it is the only way we know how to help ourselves.

The following pages describe our pain, our flaws, our rage, and our courage. While none of the characters in this book are actual clients, each is a composite based on the very real stories of the very real people who have shared their lives with me.

In the development of the Messiah concepts, I would like to thank Dr. Jay Adams and the staff at Patton State Hospital for their enthusiastic cooperation in the audiotape project. A very special appreciation is extended to the ten men who participated in the audiotape project. My life was deeply affected by hearing their stories. I am in awe of their courage, moved by their tears, grateful for their openness.

I want to thank Steve Hawthorne, who first called me a "Messiah," for unknowingly providing a key symbol for the concept of this book; I am grateful to Joel Miller, who for over twenty years has been my soul mate; a warm and heartfelt appreciation goes to Bobette Buster, whose faith in the project and support of my journey has undergirded me throughout the writing and publishing process; my deep appreciation goes to Cathy Smith and Bob Parsons who have challenged my creativity and helped hone my ideas; I am especially grateful to Paula Neal, a faithful companion, who has provided practical, down-to-earth support in my journey to break free from the Messiah Trap; I am thankful for Yang Shim Chang, whose insight has helped to open my eyes to myself, her tenacity has helped to strengthen my own, and her quick wit has kept me laughing; my special thanks to Ruth Bullock, who since my childhood has loved and nurtured me. It was Ruth who first asked me to audiotape some of my ideas so that she could share them with a friend, Tim Hansel, and it was Tim who first recognized, "Hey, there's a book here!"; I am most appreciative to Rosa and Steve Cary whose contribution was vitally important to me in the early stages of my understanding; I thank Rebecca J. Laird who has contributed to many facets of this project; I also want to thank Christine M. Anderson for her enthusiastic assistance during the final year of this project.

Many people have provided emotional and spiritual support through the years of developing this manuscript. Special thanks go to my therapists, Dr. Otto Mueller and Dr. Joan Overturf; to Rev. Ron Benefiel, Los Angeles First Church of the Nazarene and those who supported my work with children; to the prayer group: Nellie-Pearl Salsbury, Pam Els-Tracy, Cheryl Price, Lynda Jo

Branca, Ron Salsbury, Cathi Salsbury and their celebration of life, Jeffrey; to my dear friends Michael Christensen, Linda Ebeling, Rene Chansler, Dan Psaute, Mark Baker, Mark Potter, Bill Yauk, Gail Walker, Catherine Gould, Pat Luehrs, Joe Palacios, Victor Parra, Steve Ambrose, Nancy Benun, Manny Ocampo, and Jim Wilson; and to George Eckart and the Thursday night Kinship Group.

I want to express my sincere gratitude to my editor and friend, Roy M. Carlisle. When I originally presented by "Messiah" ideas, Roy caught a vision of a manuscript that was even larger than my own. He was willing to commit to the process required for the cultivation of this first-time author. With patience and insight, Roy has provided hours of consultation and assistance. He has been willing to read and evaluate outline after outline, rewrite after rewrite. It is accurate to say that his contribution has been essential.

While I am most appreciative of Roy's contribution to the development of the manuscript, I am even more grateful for his contribution to my emotional and spiritual growth. As a friend, Roy has introduced me to ideas, authors and experiences that have deepened my capacity to grow. He has understood the intensity of my feelings and has allowed me the freedom to express those feelings. Roy has proven to be a reliable friend, has taught me valuable lessons and has provided me with an abundance of support and acceptance.

Finally I would like to express gratitude to God, from whom I experience a love that transforms my life. As I have struggled through the issues related to the Messiah Trap, I have felt myself being moved forward by God's love, toward healing, the enjoyment of life, and an enlarged capacity for intimacy. In my darkest moments, I sense His presence. I am grateful for the individuals who have been led into my life, those who remind me that I am not alone.

Professional Consultation

Special thanks to my colleagues who have assisted in the development of this book through professional consultation. Each of these individuals have made a unique contribution by taking the time to review the manuscript in its various stages and then to risk providing me with an honest evaluation. I deeply appreciate the many conversations, the helpful suggestions, and the unwavering support I have received from these colleagues:

Steve Ambrose, Ph.D.
Mark Baker, Ph.D.
Ruth Bullock, Ph.D.
Jon Conte, Ph.D.
George Eckart, M.Div.
Esther Gillies, L.C.S.W.
Catherine Gould, Ph.D.
Toni Johnson, Ph.D.
Pat Luehrs, L.C.S.W.
Elizabeth Mowry
Paula Neal, M.S.W.
Joseph Palacios, M.F.C.C.
Victor Parra, L.C.S.W.
Robert Parsons, Ph.D.
Catherine Smith, Ph.D.

1. What Is the Messiah Trap?

Do you spend most of your time helping others?
> "Excuse me, but would you do me a small favor?"

> "Would you mind helping me with this?"

> "Oh, there's one last thing I'd like to ask you to do . . ."

Are you someone who helps even through the hard times?
> "I don't know what I would do without you. You've seen me through so many difficult days."

> "Through all this you have never complained. I admire how patient you are with me."

> "I'm so scared. Please don't leave me."

But do you find that there are times when you just don't have enough time for yourself?
> "I know it's your day off, but this is an emergency."

> "Whom else could I turn to? I need to see you right away."

> "This won't take very long. I'm really counting on you."

I can recall a time when I took care of everybody but myself. As the program coordinator of a community-based prevention and outreach program, my day was filled with working with clients, writing funding proposals for new projects, designing and leading parenting programs, presenting child abuse prevention techniques to children in local grade schools, chairing interagency youth committees, and lobbying for children's rights with the city council. In the evening, I would drive twenty miles into Los Angeles where I provided therapy through a church counseling center. When my last counseling session ended at 10 P.M., I then met with other church staff to work on fundraising projects such as developing multimedia presentations and writing funding proposals. Often our meetings ran until 2 A.M. It was not uncommon for me to arrive home exhausted in the early hours of morning. My life revolved around meeting the needs of others. There was something inside of me, an unknown driving force, which kept me working long hours, nearly seven days a week. I never seemed to have any time for myself, except to collapse periodically. I felt so compelled to help others that, at times, I felt like a "helpaholic."

I had fallen into the Messiah Trap.

If you are a person who spends most of your time helping others while your own needs often get pushed to the side, you also may be caught in the Messiah Trap.

Many people are caught in the Messiah Trap—administrators and aunties, mothers and ministers, social workers and secretaries. Messiahs can be found fundraising for important causes, carefully listening to clients, intensely praying with parishioners. When the children need carpooling to their music lessons, Messiahs are warming up the stationwagon. Some Messiahs wear beepers so that patients can call at any hour, some speak before large audiences, motivating them to action; others quietly visit the dying in dark hospital rooms. Messiahs are relied on to stay late at the office to finish up a needed report and to rise early to make sure everyone has a healthy lunch prepared for school.

Messiahs try to be helpful wherever they go. Many Messiahs chose professions that focus on the welfare of others, such as the ministry, social work, education, medicine, psychology, or child care. Others, such as homemakers, students, and senior adults volunteer for a variety of caregiving projects. Wherever Messiahs can be found, you can be sure they will be busy taking care of other people.

It is easy for Messiahs to become so busy taking care of other people, however, that they don't take care of themselves. In the busyness of the day, Messiahs may not even notice that their needs are going unmet. In fact, it is easy for Messiahs to pretend that they have no needs or inner hurts. Messiahs present themselves to the world as people with answers while ignoring the questions still nagging inside, as people who can give comfort while neglecting the pain throbbing deep within.

These are some Messiahs I've met.

Elizabeth is the principal of a prestigious private school. Even though she is only twenty-eight, Elizabeth's talent and dedication were quickly recognized, and she moved rapidly up the organizational ladder. With her warm smile and wise-beyond-her-years approach to management, Elizabeth won the devotion of the faculty, students, and their parents. Elizabeth prides herself on being an administrator who maintains contact with her students. Her door is always open; her office is always full of eager young students.

In spite of the fullness of her life, Elizabeth is secretly lonely. She struggles with fatigue, as her job often keeps her busy six, sometimes seven, days a week. Elizabeth watches the young mothers pick their children up after school and wonders if she will ever have the chance to have her own family. Where will she meet a man to marry when everyone in her life is somehow connected to the school? Elizabeth feels frightened, exhausted, and trapped in her desire to please everyone but herself.

Dale is a successful attorney specializing in family law. A tall, energetic, and outgoing man, Dale greets everyone with an enthusiastic handshake. In his late thirties, Dale credits his thriving law practice to the "humane" way he treats his clients. He criticizes the traditional constraints set up between professionals and clients, choosing to make himself available to clients after hours if they are in trouble.

Not only does Dale specialize in family law, he also specializes in crises. Dale rescues one client after another, dashes from one problem situation to the next. It is common for clients to call Dale in the middle of the night sobbing in grief or spewing their rage. Many of Dale's plans are interrupted by a client's crisis. Dale wants to help, but there are times when he feels confused, frustrated, and exhausted by all the demands placed upon him. He can't figure out what he's doing wrong.

Diedre is a talented counselor who juggles a case load of clients, a marriage of twenty-two years, the care of her aging mother, and the needs of her three grown children and grandchildren. Gregarious, sensitive, and warm, Diedre welcomes everyone she meets into her family. She offers a listening ear and a cup of tea to all who need her.

Diedre is becoming aware of a hard-to-define feeling that is growing within her. When she has been up half the night with a suicidal client or forced to cancel a day off to listen to a friend despair over divorce, she feels tired and frustrated. When someone asks her how she is, she just says "fine," not because she is feeling well, but because she no longer knows how she feels. She is so caught up in counseling others she has no time for herself. When did she leave herself behind? Is it too late to find herself and her own life?

Alicia is a young single mother who supports her children on the minimal salary she makes working at a preschool. Even though her finances are limited, Alicia is always helping out other people. She can be counted on to bring homemade cookies to the potluck dinner, bags of canned goods for the food drive, and colorfully wrapped Christmas presents to the foster children in town. As long as there's food on her table she is willing to share it.

What others don't see behind Alicia's broad smile and generosity are sad eyes that cry alone. Alicia so deeply feels the pain of others that she wants to give more than she is able. She feels guilty if she spends any money on herself because it's money she can't spend on her children. She chastises herself for spending money on her children that she should send to the starving children she saw on TV. No matter how much she gives, Alicia cannot seem to feel she's given enough. The more Alicia gives, however, the more frustrated she becomes.

Paul is a pastor who, over the years, has become known and respected for his compelling yet compassionate preaching style. People are drawn to Paul by the depth of his caring and his ability to deal with every situation. Paul has everything under control.

Intent on protecting people from themselves, Paul is confused by the negative reactions he sometimes receives. Paul cares deeply for others and can't understand why his efforts aren't appreciated or rewarded. Even his wife is becoming angry when he tries to help her. In fact, she is so angry these days, he's afraid she may leave him. He's doing the right thing by helping others, so why are things such a mess?

Gary is a popular public speaker and university professor. Nationally known for his insight and lively performances, Gary draws huge crowds wherever he goes. Success came easily and early for Gary. Now he feels driven to compete with his own success.

Driven by the belief that his teaching will help many, Gary's life has become a blur of airports and taxis and faceless crowds. Unable to refuse a request, Gary's schedule is overbooked and his mind overtaxed. Fits of anxiety rob him of sleep. He's afraid that he's slipping in popularity. Old presentations are renamed and re-cycled, since Gary no longer has the time to create new ones. There's no time for new ideas, no time to think, and certainly no time to feel.

James is a social worker and agency administrator. He and his wife are totally dedicated to social justice and to living a simple way of life. Side by side, they work long hours of their causes. People in their community marvel at their dedication, their compassion, and their willingness to take a stand regardless of the cost.

James's dedication to the crusade is so intense that he is becoming angrier and angrier. Enraged by the injustice he sees, frustrated by the lack of resources and support, James often struggles to contain his angry impulses. One day blurs into the next as he faces one battle after the next. He is afraid to admit that there are days when he wants to dump responsibility and wisk his wife off to a quiet and safe place. But instead he just places one foot in front of the other. Even if he wanted to leave, he sees no real way out.

These Messiahs neglect themselves because they feel that they are supposed to sacrifice their own well-being for the sake of others. This is the Messiah definition of love. Messiahs view life as a series of choices—choices between their needs and the needs of others. It is as if the Messiah believes that there is only a limited amount of nurturance, caring, and love to go around—only enough for everyone else but nothing left over for the Messiah.

Consequently, there can grow inside of a Messiah a gnawing, hard-to-describe feeling. Sometimes it feels like being underappreciated for sacrifices made. Other times it feels more like guilt when taking time for personal needs somehow means having to disappoint or neglect someone else. Many times the feeling is fatigue, a deep tiredness that seems too heavy to carry. Most often Messiahs are too busy to feel anything at all except for the pressure of having too much to do and too little time.

When Messiahs feel overwhelmed and underappreciated, most respond by helping even more. Caught up with the idea that addressing their own pain is "selfish," most Messiahs are encouraged to help others, not themselves. Through our churches, families, and the society at large, Messiahs are usually taught to deal with inner feelings of deprivation by becoming a "cheerful giver", to fight their own depression by helping those who are worse off than themselves. Very few stop and question their way of seeing the world and themselves in it.

This book challenges the beliefs that have lured so many into the Messiah Trap.

WHAT IS THE MESSIAH TRAP?

The Messiah Trap is a lie that is deadly and deceiving. It is a two-sided lie that, on the surface, appears to be noble and godly and gracious. After all, being a caring and helpful person is something we value. But the Messiah Trap is not what it appears to be.

SIDE 1: "IF I DON'T DO IT, IT WON'T GET DONE"

Several years ago I found some stationery on which was drawn a sad-faced dog looking like it had been flattened by a steamroller. The caption read, "If I don't do it, it won't get done."

This message is the first side of the two-sided Messiah Trap. Messiahs have been taught (and therefore believe) that the primary purpose in life is to help other people. If the Messiah does not help them, no one else will. It is the Messiah's responsibility to help Daddy stop drinking, to keep the office running smoothly, to reach out to that teenager no one else seems to like. The Messiah feels responsible for making sure that everything turns out right and that everybody's happy. It is the Messiah's job, and the Messiah's alone.

SIDE 2: "EVERYONE ELSE'S NEEDS TAKE PRIORITY OVER MINE"

With so many people depending on the Messiah, so the lie goes, all must be made right in the world before the Messiah's needs can be addressed. This is the second side of the Messiah Trap: "Everyone else's needs take priority over mine." Messiahs are expected to put everyone else first.

Believing the second side of the Messiah Trap makes it terribly difficult to take care of one's own legitimate needs. Attempts at self-nurturing are often seen as "selfish" and being selfish is probably the worst grievance a Messiah could commit.

When you fall into the Trap, you are caught in the snare of two contrasting (and false) ideas about yourself. The Messiah, on one hand, feels the weight of tremendous responsibility for others and consequently becomes the most important person in the world. The Messiah feels indispensable. Yet, on the other hand, the Messiah often feels unimportant, as personal needs do not seem to merit any concern. It is common for Messiahs to feel isolated, with no one to turn to when the pain becomes intolerable. As a Messiah, you may busy taking care of others but find that no one is busy taking care of you. The Messiah Trap is an odd combination of feeling grandiose yet worthless, of being needed and yet abandoned, of playing God while groveling.

It is my belief that, as children of God, we are *all* valuable, we *all* warrant nurturance and protection . . . even the Messiah. The needs of one are no less important than the needs of another. To view love as merely being the sacrifice of one for another is to misunderstand love in its totality. Love is balanced and fair, nonexploitive, caring, and strong. There is no competition between lovers, no choice between one or the other, because love is full and whole and large enough to encompass us all.

I urge you, if you are caught in the Messiah Trap, to stop long enough to read through the following pages. Be warned, your view of yourself and of love may be challenged. You may have been taught a distorted view of relationships and caring that has left you chained to a self-damaging, addictive way of life. Many Messiahs have been raised to believe that the lies of the Trap are actually God-given, based in scripture and church tradition. It may take a great deal of courage to question such fundamental beliefs, but I encourage you to read on—to learn about what it is like to be a Messiah, caught in the Messiah Trap and how many are breaking free.

2. Can There Be a Hidden Trap in a "Happy" Childhood?

"So you want me to tell you about my childhood, huh? It was such a long time ago, and besides, mine was a happy childhood. I'm afraid you're going to be very disappointed. No beatings, no rapes, just a good family always there to help other people out when they needed a hand."

—DIEDRE

Since Diedre first called for counseling—"nothing major, just to straighten out a few things in my mind,"—I found her bright and enthusiastic. A therapist with a thriving private practice, the mother of three grown children, the wife of an engineer, and the caretaker of her elderly mother, she often found herself torn between competing responsibilities. "I just need to find some time for myself," she announced as the first meeting commenced, "and when I do get time, I want to have a better idea of who I am. Somehow I've gotten lost in everyone else's life."

In order to better understand how Diedre lost herself along the way, we were beginning to look into her past, back into her childhood to locate how she became trapped by the two Messiah lies. Assuring me that no such trap existed in her childhood, she proceeded to describe her parents.

"Both my parents were kind, giving people. My mother took care of us when we were little, of course. My dad owned his own business, which did pretty well through the Depression. At least, we seemed to have more money than most. He seemed to spend more time at the church, however, than at the office—being on the church board, teaching Sunday School, and always busy helping out. Sometimes, when things got bad for some of the other families in the church, they would pack all of us up in the car and drive from home to home so Mom could deliver hot meals." Diedre smiled with pride. "Yes, my parents were good people."

"Were most of your family gatherings centered around helping someone else?"

Diedre nodded, "Hmm . . . yes, I guess they were. We didn't go on too many family vacations or anything like that. Most of our time and money went to the church or to some worthy cause."

She paused, "You know, now that I think of it, we hardly ever had a meal without inviting someone else to share it. Like I said, times were hard on most people and kinder to us. But one time my younger brother, Sidney, was showing off, trying to get some attention, I suppose, and my mother said, 'Shape up, young man. We have company.'

"He snapped back, 'We always have company! When can it just be us?'

"My parents stared at him in alarm. 'I don't want to hear talk like that, Son,' my father growled at him. I think he was madder then than I had ever seen him. 'You be thankful for what you have. I am ashamed that you would be so selfish. We'll talk about this again later!' Sid shrank back into his chair, surprised at Dad's anger.

"After our guests left for the evening, my father gathered us up in the living room. 'I don't ever want to hear one of you be so rude in front of our guests. Is that any way to thank God for all He has given us?' Looking at Sid, he demanded, 'Do you want me to turn people away when they are hungry?'

"Sid dropped his head and whispered, 'No.' 'Who is going to feed them if we don't?' my father continued. Sid shrugged his little shoulders.

" 'Didn't you think about how you would hurt their feelings?' Sid's curly head shook no. Directing his gaze back to all of us, my dad declared, 'I expect you to think about other people's feelings for a change. Never again do I want to be embarrassed like that, do you hear me?' We all did.

"I felt so ashamed . . . and guilty, too, I suppose. After all, God had been so good to us and we were acting like selfish little children."

When asked what she had done that was selfish, Diedre replied, "Well, *I* hadn't done anything, really. And Sid was just trying to get someone to notice him. He wasn't really acting out or anything." A frown came over her attractive face. "We were expected to be quiet and giving. Nothing less was tolerated.

"I remember sitting in church, looking at the other families with the fathers unemployed and the mothers doing odd jobs, just trying to pull together the next meal and I felt so, so. . . ." She stopped.

"Responsible?" I ventured.

"Yes, exactly! Like it was up to us to take care of the others."

"Diedre, now that you are an adult, do you believe you caused the financial problems of those families?"

"Of course not," she responded quickly.

"Did you and your family have the resources to restore the economy?" I asked.

She looked up with an irritated gaze. "We were trying to help, not save the nation."

"Is that how it felt to you as a little girl? Did you feel responsible for the care of every person you knew?"

Diedre leaned back into the couch. "Sure I did. I always felt responsible. I did then, and I do now. If it didn't sound so absurd, I think I would admit that somewhere down deep I really felt that I and my family were supposed to stop all that pain—a bit grandiose, isn't it?"

Her eyes crinkled at the edges as she smiled slightly, "So that's how I learned the first side of the Messiah Trap. It is one thing to want to help but it is quite another to take on the responsibility for the well-being of all those families."

"And the second side?" I inquired.

"I learned that *my* needs were not to be addressed; in fact, they were a source of embarrassment to my parents. It's beginning to make sense to me—why I feel so responsible now for my clients, my children, for Ed, and my mother. No wonder I feel so uncomfortable trying to tell them what I need. I'm afraid I'll be chastised like Sid was."

Diedre, like so many Messiahs, grew up in a Messiah home, raised by parents who believed the lies of the Messiah Trap. She was taught, through the well-intended example of her parents, a distorted view of what it means to love other people. If she had been raised in a non-Messiah home, she would have learned that the needs of the children and the parents are of equal importance to the needs of those outside the home. Attention would have been given to each child, each adult. There would have been times to open the door to those in need, as well as times to shut the door tightly in order to protect and care for those inside.

In a Messiah home like Diedre's, however, the door is always open. Diedre was led to believe that it was the responsibility of her and her family to help *every* person in need. This was a tremendous load for one family to carry—if they didn't help those in need, no one else would. People would starve and God would be displeased. (Side 1: "If I don't do it, it won't get done").

Diedre's family did not share with others in a way that could address the legitimate needs of *all* people involved. Even though Diedre's parents were "helpaholics," they were addicted to helping *other* people. This is a typical trait of Messiahs. When a Messiah helps, only some people are selected. Others are ignored. Consequently, the needs of Diedre and her siblings were disregarded, their safety unprotected, and their value understated. Furthermore, Diedre's parents taught their children that God was not at all interested in their needs. Whenever Diedre and her siblings felt the need for attention and nurturance from their parents, they were labeled "selfish" and an "embarrassment." Through these subtle but powerful words, Diedre was set up for the second side of the Messiah Trap: "Everyone else's needs take priority over mine."

Were Diedre's parents intending to be cruel to and withholding from their children? Not at all. Were they insensitive? Uncaring? These terms would not apply. Rather, her parents were people who cared a great deal about the suffering they saw around them, especially in a time when pain and discouragement were in such abundance. But regardless of their intent to heal, the impact on the children was detrimental. Diedre had grown up in a good home but was, unfortunately, raised by parents who had fallen into the Messiah Trap.

Parents, like Diedre's, who are caught in the Messiah Trap tend to raise their children to be "little" Messiahs. Little Messiahs are trained, from the earliest years, to feel responsible for the well-being of others (Side 1: "If I don't do it, it won't get done") but not to expect their own needs to be met (Side 2: "Everyone else's needs take priority over mine.")

BEING PLACED IN MESSIAH ROLES AS CHILDREN

I want to state very clearly that *children have legitimate needs.* This truth may seem self-evident, but in my counseling experience and observation it's a truth often disregarded. In order for us to grow into adults who are capable of loving ourselves and others, able to bond in mutually caring relationships, sensitive to but not overwhelmed by the needs of others, we need to master each childhood stage of development. As infants, we require protection and nurturance in order to learn how to trust. Young children, moving out to explore the world, need a structured but flexible home environment. While it is appropriate to give children more responsibility as they mature, *it is crucial that children be allowed to be children throughout their childhood years.*

The natural flow of development is disrupted, however, if a child is forced to "grow up" too fast by being placed in adult caregiving roles prematurely. Diedre, like many Messiahs, was an adult who never quite had a childhood. It was taken from her so quietly and subtly that she never even noticed that her "happy" childhood was a non- existent childhood.

THE LITTLE PARENT

"I was the first-born, with three more after me. My youngest sister, Andrea, is about to get married— finally!" Diedre grinned. "Actually, I think of her as being more like my own child than my sister. I was the one who raised her once my mom went to work. I helped out a lot when I was pretty young, actually. Both of my parents were always so busy helping out at church and all, I guess I ended up taking care of us at home. I was always babysitting someone, it seemed."

"The first time I babysat, I suppose I was around five years old or so. Mom needed to take some groceries over to a neighbor who was ill, and she left me 'in charge' of Sid. He must have been three then."

"I remember feeling pretty scared. But also sort of proud of the fact that she trusted me to be so grown up. It made me feel good to be 'Mama's helper.' I helped with the cooking and the cleaning.

I never remember playing with my brothers and sisters. There was so much work to do. After a while I just didn't feel like one of them anymore. I became more of a disciplinarian or a counselor than a sister.''

As Diedre spoke it became more clear how she had been robbed of the opportunity to be a child—a child who was free to play and tease and enjoy natural, age-appropriate relationships with her siblings. There was a void left when her parents attended to the needs of others but neglected to attend to their own children. Like so many Messiahs, Diedre moved into that void by taking on a parental role.

She took on the responsibility of caring for her siblings (if she didn't do it, it wouldn't have been done) and thereby sacrificed her own childhood needs (the needs of her parents and siblings took priority over hers). Diedre became the "Little Parent."

While Diedre was the eldest of four, not all Messiahs are first-born. Often the older child is given too much responsibility too soon, but children of any birth order can be caught in the Messiah Trap. What is required is that children, regardless of age or birth order, be taught the lies of the Messiah Trap and expected to perform adult caregiving roles while they are still children.

PEER OF THE PARENT

"If you didn't play with your brother or sisters, did you have friends your own age?"

"Oh, sure," Diedre responded. "Our neighborhood was full of kids, and most of them seemed to spend all their time at our house. Since I was usually watching my siblings, Mom just put me in charge of them all."

When I asked whom she confided in, Diedre replied, "If I talked with anyone, it was my mom. I felt rather special at times because it felt like she treated me more like a friend than a daughter."

"Sometimes I liked it. Other times not." Diedre looked away as a shadow covered her usually open face. Slowly she explained, "We really were a happy family—I mean, happier than most. But there were times when my dad would be out at some meeting or helping out somewhere, and I guess my mom got lonely at times.

It wasn't like he was abusive to her or anything. He wasn't out drinking or something like that. He just wasn't home very much.''

Diedre described how she, as a young girl, propped up in one of their hard kitchen chairs, strained to keep awake as her mother complained about her neglectful husband. "Night after night my mother cornered me and would go on and on and on. It didn't seem to matter to her that I was just a little girl or that I had school the next morning.'' Diedre paused again, uncomfortable with the emotions she was experiencing.

"Sometimes I felt mad at her,'' Diedre continued. "After all, Dad was out helping people. I thought we were supposed to be 'cheerful givers.' But I also dreaded him leaving at night after dinner because he left her with me. Mostly I felt bad for her because *I* missed him too. I would've done anything to make her happy but no matter what I did, it never seemed to quite work.''

Diedre became a peer to her mother, thereby suffering yet another violation of her childhood. Not only was she robbed of her rightful relationships with her siblings and the opportunity to develop friendships with children her own age, she was forced to befriend her mother. This little girl was not developmentally ready to be an adult—she was a child—and yet she was expected to perform as an adult, as the "Peer to the Parent.''

It is no surprise to find that Diedre, as an adult, still lends a listening ear to everyone she meets. Wherever she goes, regardless of her level of fatigue, she feels compelled to sit and listen to every person who has a story to tell, a question to ask, or a comment to make. She is still acting like the little girl, who, in an attempt to fill the emotional void left by her father, was entrapped by her mother's illegitimate demands.

SURROGATE SPOUSE

While the Peer of the Parent role may occur between a parent and child of the same gender, the Surrogate Spouse role usually develops between a parent and child of opposite gender. A child becomes a Surrogate Spouse when one parent bonds with the child as a substitute for the spouse or as a supplement to the marriage.

I asked how often she saw her father. Diedre explained, "Actually, I think I saw him more than my mother did. I was always his favorite. Some nights he would take me with him, to meetings and to the neighbors' houses. I remember feeling so proud and pretty sitting next to him, listening to him help the others. Everywhere we went, people were glad to see him. I'd think, 'That's my dad.'

"As I got older, he started confiding in me about how things were going with the business, and with him. Especially during the rough times, he'd say, 'Now don't upset your mother with this. You know how easily troubled she can get.' And then he'd go into detail about some problem or another." Diedre smiled warily. "I don't know if I'm proud or embarrassed by telling you this. He always treated me as if I were stronger than the others, even stronger than my mom."

The relationship that develops between a parent and the child (the Surrogate Spouse role) is a deep emotional bond, one that seems to eclipse the connection between spouses. While no sexual involvement occurs, the impact on the child on an emotional level is similar to that of incest. In both incest and Surrogate Spouse cases, the child is expected to perform as an adult. In incest, the performance is sexual. The Surrogate Spouse is expected to provide nurturance and intimacy well beyond the natural capabilities of a child. The young Messiah is forced to relate on an adult level.

The roles of Surrogate Spouse and Peer of the Parent are similar in that the child is placed in a peer relationship with one or both of the parents. As all young Messiahs placed in such positions, the child is expected to provide for the parent's needs because no one is available to do so ("Your father is out doing the Lord's work. Won't you stay up with me tonight, and we'll talk?"—Side 1). In the process, the child's needs are disregarded ("Oh, you can stay up a little longer. You're such a big help." Side 2).

Many adult Messiahs began as young children who were trained to act as their parents' peers. Most often, this mismatch occurs in families where one parent is consistently busy and thereby emotionally absent from the home. This can include families, for example, where a workaholic mother is employed during the day and going to night school (busy with volunteer work, out helping a sick friend, at a committee meeting). The father may turn to his daughter to fill his time. This can also include the wife who bonds with her son (Surrogate Spouse) or daughter (Peer of the Parent) to supplement what she misses when her (evangelist, truck driver, salesman, public speaker, pilot) husband is gone for weeks at a stretch. The emotionally absent parent may be out doing good things for others (having also fallen into the Messiah Trap), which often makes the child feel even more obligated to "help" out at home with the neglected parent. The impact on the child is devastating.

CAN THERE BE A HIDDEN TRAP IN A "HAPPY" CHILDHOOD?

Can there be a hidden trap in a "happy" childhood? There certainly can be.

Diedre struggled as she came to see how her godly, well-meaning parents had presented her with a distorted view of love, God, and of her place in the world. She had been a "good" girl, which, in essence, meant that she had no opportunity to be a girl at all. Like most Messiahs, at a very young age she became an adult. Deidre had been pulled into the Messiah Trap, not by someone cruel, but by her own parents, who were themselves victims of the Messiah Trap.

It is often very difficult to discern the damage incurred by children who have been raised in such Messiah households. Like Diedre, many Messiahs have grown up with the belief that childhood was a positive experience and that the values held are sound, even God-given. It can be very troubling to entertain the thought that perhaps one's own childhood, while peaceful enough, was nevertheless stolen by people who meant no harm.

Most Messiahs choose to pretend to have a happy childhood when in fact they had little, if any, childhood at all. As long as this pretense continues, the Messiah will remain caught in the Messiah Trap. While Messiahs are driven, on an unconscious level, toward the healing of those childhood wounds, resolution is difficult because Messiahs have never been given permission even to identify legitimate needs, let alone address those needs. But these needs will not remain invisible simply because the Messiah does not have eyes to see, nor will the pain be silent because the

Messiah turns a deaf ear to the cries. The unidentified needs and unresolved pain of childhood become hidden motivations in everything the adult Messiah does. It takes courage to discern the truth about one's childhood, yet it is a necessary step in breaking free of the Messiah Trap.

3. How Messiahs Are Trapped Through Childhood Trauma

> Sure, I've had some rough things happen in my childhood, but that doesn't affect me now. I'm not out hurting other people. I try to help everyone I meet!
>
> —JAMES

I have come to believe that Messiahs help other people in an attempt to help themselves. Each Messiah has been hurt in some way. While the pain suffered may differ, I have found repeatedly that those who have fallen into the Messiah Trap have been wounded in some deep way as children.

Some Messiahs, as described previously, were placed in adult caregiving roles prematurely. Many others, however, have suffered serious childhood trauma that has been inadequately resolved. Some Messiah children have been torn between parents in marital disputes. Others have suffered from the turbulence that results when a mother or father abuses drugs or alcohol. Some Messiahs were once children who were seriously neglected and left to parent themselves. Still others carry emotional and physical scars from beatings or sexual assault.

CHILDREN OF FAMILIES WITH MARITAL PROBLEMS

The four people sitting in my office were obviously in a great deal of emotional pain. Paul, a minister known for his enthusiastic preaching style, was now sitting, hands clinched, glaring at the floor. Two of his daughters, aged four and six, huddled together on the couch, sniffling quietly. Sally, the six-year-old, periodically patted her younger sister Robin on the knee. Tami, the eldest at nine, had pulled her chair between her parents. All were listening to Cindi, their mother, sob out her frustration regarding their troubled marriage.

"I married late, as you know. I wanted to make sure I didn't make a mistake. Ha! What a fool I was." Cindi complained.

Tami glanced at her father as Paul's shoulders sagged. Turning sorrowful eyes toward her mother, she pleaded, "Please don't say things like that. You're hurting Daddy."

Cindi continued undaunted. "At first I liked all the attention he paid me, but soon it became suffocating. Always fussing over me like I was some fragile doll—trying to take care of me. I began to think, 'I've got to get out of here. I can't breathe!' I was just about ready to leave him, and then I found out I was pregnant." She looked over at her husband. "We decided to try to make it work, you know, for the children."

Parents who claim to stay in unhappy marriages "for the sake of the children" may feel they are illustrating how much they care for their children's welfare. They may, however, be deeply wounding their children by giving them an inflated view of their power and responsibility. These children are told indirectly that the continuation of the family unit ultimately lies in their hands. If it were not for the children, the family would dissolve. Translated into the lie of the Messiah Trap, the child receives the message that if the child doesn't keep the family together, then no one else will (Side 1: "If I don't do it, it won't get done").

It is not uncommon for children placed in this position to feel overwhelmed by a sense of responsibility. Rather than being responsible for their families, however, children are in fact dependent on their families. Abandonment could mean death. Children know and fear this fact. Ensuring the continuation of the family unit, then, can become paramount to ensuring their own survival. I have observed that these children often live with the fear that, should they make some mistake, the family and their fragile security would shatter.

Another aspect to this message is equally as damaging. Since the parents are supposedly staying together "because of the children," the continuation of the marriage can become a source of guilt for these young ones. It is clear that the parents are unhappy. This is no family secret. But why do their parents endure such unhappiness? "Because of the children." It is understandable, then, that little Robin, Sally and Tami would feel guilty—since they seem to be the cause of so much pain and hardship. If they had never been born, perhaps their parents could have been happy.

Cindi continued to spew her rage, "We did try, of course. At least I did. But things have just gone from bad to worse." Robin crawled up into her mother's lap and pushed her stuffed bunny toward Cindi's face. "Oh, thank you, honey," Cindi acknowledged her youngest daughter's offering. In Robin's little-girl attempt to comfort and please her mother, the Messiah Trap was being set for this child. Robin was learning that her needs were secondary to those of the adults in her life (Side 2: "Everyone else's needs take priority over mine").

"Please play with your toys on the couch, dear," Cindi instructed Robin as she sent her away. Dragging her bunny behind her, Robin obeyed. Welcoming her little sister with comforting arms, Sally cuddled and cooed over Robin. Beneath the drone of Cindi's voice, I could hear Sally whispering quietly, "It's OK, Robin. Don't be scared." Sally was also becoming a Messiah by taking on an adult caregiving role when she herself was needing comfort.

Finally Paul spoke up. "Things have been difficult. No one is denying that. There's been fault on both sides."

Cindi demanded, "Are you telling me this is my fault?"

"That's not what he meant, Mom," Tami said in a voice well beyond her years. "He wasn't trying to blame you."

Pulling her sweater around her, Cindi insisted, "Well, he'd better not try! You can just tell your father he'd better not try!"

Perched precariously between her parents, Tami tried to soften the verbal blows, interpret the messages, and negotiate a compromise. Tami was given no opportunity to express her own fears, disappointments, or anger. She dared not. Her family could crumble if she weren't there to orchestrate some order. Tami's childhood was being spent, not being a child, but in preparation for becoming a Messiah.

Drawing children into marital disputes places a tremendous responsibility on shoulders too young and weak to carry such a load. And in the case of divorce, the children often come to believe that they, by making some mistake, have utterly failed. Robin may struggle with shame over her inability to please her parents, while Sally may suffer from guilt over her failure to protect Robin from such a loss. As the family splits into two households, it can be expected that Tami will also be split between her loyalties, used by both her parents to send messages back and forth, as throughout her childhood years she acts as a conduit for her parents' rage.

The truth of the matter is that children do not have the power to keep a marriage together nor to break it up. Marriages continue or end according to the needs of the parents. Paul and Cindi had stayed together for a variety of reasons, reasons that came out in further sessions. These included the need for financial security, the fear of living alone, and even the need to be unhappy. During this session, however, Paul and Cindi were not willing to take responsibility for their choices. It was much easier for them to claim that the unhappiness was endured for some noble cause—for the sake of the children—even though this claim was made at their children's expense.

CHILDREN OF SUBSTANCE-ABUSING FAMILIES

"I felt it was my job to keep my dad from drinking," Gary explained. "I don't know why I thought I could get him to stop. Mom never had been able to, but I kept hoping."

"My father was one of the most outgoing, robust men. He could stand up in front of a group of people and have them laughing for hours. When he was sober, he was a great father. Took me fishing, played football, you know, the whole bit." Darkness fell across his face, "But before long the drinking would start again and it was, well, just awful. A nightmare of violence and broken promises."

Children who are raised by parents who are addicted to drugs or alcohol must contend with a turbulent and unpredictable world. The chaotic nature of the home creates an arena where the child's development is disrupted in unpredictable spurts. At times Gary's legitimate needs were acknowledged and addressed. Then, with no warning, these needs would be suddenly disregarded. Gary learned how to survive amid the chaos, danger, and disappointment by denying his own needs (Side 2) and by taking care of his father and even by taking on the responsibilities of "father" (Side 1).

"As soon as I could, maybe I was around seven or eight. I started working odd jobs after school while Mom took care of the younger kids. I didn't feel like I had much of a choice. Mom did what she could, but if I hadn't kept some money coming in, somebody probably would have come and put all us kids into foster care. I had to hold things together. My dad certainly wouldn't" (Side 1).

"I used to dread hearing my dad's unsteady footsteps come up the stairs. He could be so abusive, especially to my mother. I tried to protect her and the others." He paused. "There was only one thing I feared more than having my dad come home drunk, and that was dreading the night when the hall would be silent. I lived in continual fear that his violent temper would someday get him killed."

Gary's childhood fear is not uncommon. All children fear abandonment. It is a universal experience for us all. But for children of alcoholic parents, this fear can become a reality. Permanent abandonment is a frighteningly real possibility. Gary's father had already abandoned consistent care for the family's emotional and physical well-being. Gary knew that each time his father left the house might be the last time he would see him.

"As I got older, though, I sort of liked being the man around the house. Mom and I got along great, and it felt good to have her depend on me. We still have a close relationship. She lives in a small apartment behind our house. Mom still depends on me." Gary discarded his childhood early and stepped into the role of father—protector, provider, companion, parent. It is common for such children to develop a co-parent role with the nonabusing parent.

Children from substance-abusing families easily fall into the Messiah Trap through several roles, by becoming the Little Parent, the Surrogate Spouse, or the Peer of the Parent. Regardless of the approach, children like Gary are taught the two sides of the Messiah Trap. If Gary hadn't taken care of his family, he believed, no one else would have (Side 1), and keeping his family together was worth anything it might cost him personally (Side 2). The hurt Gary experienced was deep and easily knocked him off balance, sending him headlong into the Messiah Trap.

NEGLECTED CHILDREN

With pain in his eyes, Dale described the years of his growing up. "I spent most of my nights as a boy huddled in alleyways or roaming the streets of Los Angeles. My mom," his voice cracked, "well, she often entertained her customers in our one room apartment but the money she earned went to support her drug habit, not me."

"It didn't take me long to learn how to fend for myself. I survived well on the streets once I got the hang of digging through garbage cans for food, how to beg, even how to steal. I was pretty slick," he confessed.

"It's a long way from the streets to law school," I observed.

Dale grinned, "One day I was trying to con this lady out of some change when this guy came up to me and offered me a job. The next thing I know he had me involved in a youth employment program through a church in our neighborhood. That guy saved my life. He even tutored me through high school and helped support me through college and law school. He tried to undo all the damage my mother had done."

It was easy to understand Dale's gratitude to the street counselor who had befriended him. I was less optimistic, however, that all the damage caused by his mother had been undone. His mother had taught Dale the lies of the Messiah Trap—that he was in charge and that he was alone. As an attorney, he seemed compelled to rescue his clients, as if he were somehow still rescuing himself from the dangers of the street.

Such severe neglect is relatively easy to spot. Many Messiahs, however, begin as neglected children whose mistreatment is hidden because the neglect is on an emotional level. Children who are provided with clothing, shelter, and life's physical necessities are rarely considered "neglected." Children, however, who are not cared for psychologically, regardless of the socio-economic status of the family, are vulnerable to falling into the Messiah Trap.

Here is a list of candidates for the Trap:

- Children from large families
- Children whose parents are physically or mentally ill, thereby unable to nurture consistently
- Children from single-parent families whose custodial parent is overwhelmed by the responsibility of raising a family and/or who rarely see their non-custodial parent

- Children in families where both parents are working and have insufficient time and energy for parenting
- Children placed in residential (boarding) schools who feel abandoned and neglected by their families

When the legitimate needs of children get lost in the overriding needs and problems of their parents, children are forced to parent themselves. These children learn that if anything is going to be done, they will have to do it (Side 1) and that their needs will certainly not be attended to by anyone else (Side 2). Admittedly, the financial pressures and time limitations experienced by parents are real. But so are the legitimate needs of children. When a parent abdicates responsibility for the emotional nurturance of a child, regardless of the "legitimacy" of the reasons, the Trap may snap shut on yet another Messiah.

PHYSICALLY ABUSED CHILDREN

James, intense and intelligent, reluctantly came to counseling after being hospitalized for an ulcer. "I don't have the time or the money for such an extravagance," he complained. But his physician insisted. "The only problem I have," James informed me, "is that there are too few hours in the day to do all that needs to be done."

When asked about the parenting he had received, James described how his mother would fly into violent fits. "Different things set her off—my room, for example. I tried to keep my room clean, but sometimes it just wasn't clean enough for her."

James clenched his powerful hands, "One time I remember I left for school without making my bed. I thought I could get home and clean up before she got home from work but I got tied up at the gym. She got there before I did, and she exploded!" Waving his arms in the air, James demonstrated, "She slapped me in the face, over and over and over. I put my arm up to protect myself, and she started screaming that I was trying to hit her! I felt so guilty. If only I had kept my room clean none of that would have happened."

Through his mother's abuse, James came to accept a distorted view of his power and responsibility. He believed that if he behaved properly (defined as pleasing his mother), then he could protect himself from harm. If he did not behave, then James would get what he must deserve—a beating. James grew up in a frightening world where his safety was shattered by the person who should have been his protector.

James learned that if his world would ever be safe, it was up to him to make it so (Side 1). His mother's abusive behavior also taught him that his needs for safety were unimportant to anyone else (Side 2). It is not surprising to find that this scared little boy spent his adolescent years lifting weights and building up his physical strength, and as adult became a dedicated man whose life is now consumed in advocating for the poor, the helpless, and homeless.

SEXUALLY ABUSED CHILDREN

"I have been dreading the day when you would ask about my past, my childhood,"—Alicia confessed as her eyes once again brimmed full of tears.

"Only proceed if you feel ready," I assured her.

Sighing heavily, Alicia announced, "Oh, I guess I'm as ready as I'll ever be" and went on to describe a family that on the surface appeared tranquil and almost perfect. "Mom had been sick on and off for years, but we all seemed to adjust to that after a while. Nights were especially difficult for her so Dad didn't always get much sleep. But we all pitched in. I tried to help out as much as I could."

"Things went OK until I was around nine. Grampa died suddenly. What a shock to all of us! I was in the kitchen cooking dinner because Mom wasn't up to it. She was back in her bedroom, and my brothers and sister were out playing in the yard. The phone rang, and I could hear Dad's voice start off sounding normal but then it got all tight." Alicia shuddered, "Even though I couldn't understand what he was saying, I could tell something was very wrong."

The tears flowed more freely as Alicia continued to tell her sad secret. "I went into the living room to see what was going on, and he was just sitting there on the couch with the strangest look on his face. It was hard to tell if he was sad or angry or what. Trying to comfort him, I sat down beside him and leaned my head up against his shoulder. I was about to ask about the phone call when he reached over and held onto me. I think he was crying. At first I felt good about him holding me. It made me feel special. But then, I don't know, it started feeling funny. I got this queasy feeling in my stomach." Her voice cracked.

"I should've made him stop! It was all my fault! He was just too upset to know what he was doing . . . " Her body shook as her secret broke free.

"He took my face in his hands and started kissing me. I'd never been kissed like that before. And then he started rubbing me all over and making me rub him." Hiding her face in her hands, she confessed, "It was so scary and awful."

"And then he just stood up and started walking away like nothing had happened. I was so stunned I sat there on the couch—in shock, I suppose. He turned around and said, 'Don't ever tell anyone about this. Especially your mother. It would kill her, you know how sick she is. Do you understand me?' I nodded. 'Besides,' he promised, 'It will never happen again.' "

Alicia shook her head slowly from side to side. "And I believed him. I never told anyone about it even though . . . even though it happened over and over and over. There must be something very bad in me to make him want to do that to his own daughter— that's what he told me, that it was my fault, that I asked for it. Maybe I did. I just don't know anymore. It just seems like a bad dream."

Children, like Alicia, who have been sexually exploited and misused, are set up for the Messiah Trap in several ways. First, children who are sexually abused often experience an exaggerated sense of responsibility and guilt. We tend, in this society, to blame the victim for the actions of the assailant, whether the person is a victim of rape ("Well, with the way you dress, you were just asking for it"), burglary ("It wouldn't have happened if you had only nailed those back windows shut like I told you"), or mugging ("Why were you out there after dark, anyway?"). Children like Alicia receive this message loud and clear: the responsible party is the child (Side 1).

Secondly, victims of sexual abuse are taught that they are to please and obey adults regardless of the cost. Alicia was taught to feel responsible for meeting her father's needs (Side 1) regardless of the sacrifice (Side 2).

Thirdly, victims of molestation are taught to distrust their own feelings and perceptions. Children are often lied to about the abuse. A grandfather may tell his stepdaughter that all little girls learn about sex this way. An aunt may tell her nephew that she has a new game that is so special and fun, they must never tell anyone else about it. Alicia was led to believe that she had somehow seduced her father, that the molestation was her fault. In such cases the child is not only violated but also told that his or her feelings about the violation are in error and not to be trusted. Alicia's confusion over who was responsible, even to doubting whether the molestation had actually occurred, is a common experience among children whose ability to trust themselves has been so tragically undermined. Such children often release any claim on protecting themselves or having their own needs addressed (Side 2).

Not only are these children deceived, but they are also coerced into deceiving others. Alicia was threatened into silence "to protect her mother's health." Abuse victims, even pre-schoolers, have been known to endure indescribable horrors rather than put their loved ones in jeopardy. Suffering abuse and keeping the abuse a secret become a way of life for these little ones.

When the molestation is kept a secret, the truth cannot be told. Lies must be told instead.

"I lied to my mother about where I went and what I did with my father." Alicia explained. "I tried to stay away from him whenever I could. 'I just don't understand it,' she would say. 'You were always Daddy's little girl.' If my mother only knew."

Lies, lies, lies. Alicia was trapped by the lies of the Messiah Trap.

Each time Alicia awoke to see her father's naked silhouette standing over her bed, she understood all to well whose needs were important (Side 2: Everyone else's needs take priority over mine"). There was no one in the house she could trust to protect her. If the abuse was ever to end, she knew that it would be up to her alone. (Side 1: "If I don't do it, it won't get done.")

TRAPPED THROUGH CHILDHOOD TRAUMA

Robin, Sally, Tami, Gary, Dale, James, and Alicia all have one thing in common—they were set up for the Messiah Trap through the trauma they suffered as children. Rather than being protected and nurtured through their tender years, these little ones were jolted, exploited, and deceived. They received slaps instead of hugs, seduction instead of safety. Childhood innocence and curiosity were replaced by the unwieldy load of adult-level responsibility and a violation that cut to the core of their self worth. In the attempt to hide the ugliness and horror, their childhood trauma was often buried as these hurting children grew into adult Messiahs—adults driven to help others who remind them of themselves, driven by the pain of their own childhoods.

4. What Are the Eight Messiah Characteristics?

Even though I'm with people most of the time I feel, well, sort of alone and even different. Maybe even a little anxious that one of them may take a good look at me and see just how out of place I really am.

—ELIZABETH

The first time I met Elizabeth, our encounter more resembled a job interview than a counseling session. Highly tailored in dress and manner, Elizabeth sat erect and confident. Only the constant wringing of her manicured hands belied her deep emotion. She waited for me to begin. "Whenever you're ready, please just tell me about yourself," I said.

She answered promptly by describing the programs at the prestigious private high school where she served as principal. When she finished, she drew in a deep breath and waited, seemingly unable to offer anything other than a well-performed presentation.

"But tell me about *you*," I asked quietly.

Tears began to well up in her eyes. "That's the whole point. Besides my work, there's nothing else to tell. I feel driven, almost addicted, to helping these students. I've always seen myself as successful, at least until now. It's my personal life, or lack of one to be more accurate. My whole life is my work. I have this feeling like I'm missing something, like there's got to be more."

When asked about her growing-up years, Elizabeth explained, "My folks split up when I was two. That was back in the days when no one got divorced and preschools wouldn't accept two-year-olds. My mother had to make special arrangements at a preschool, since she had to go to work. Mom says I cried a lot. She says I would stand sobbing at the preschool door trying to push it open with my little hands so I could follow her out to the car. But I don't remember that at all. The main thing I remember was how much I loved the crafts and games and my teacher, Miss Carlson.

"Miss Carlson let me feed the turtles, put my drawings up on the board, things like that—probably because I was so young and the only child in the class from a 'broken home.' It didn't seem broken to me, I guess because I was so little when Dad left. I don't even remember living with him at all. In fact, I have more memories of Miss Carlson and babysitters than I do of either of my parents. I know my mom did her best for me. She would say to me as she dropped me off at the school, 'Be Mother's helper and do good in school today.' So I did."

Elizabeth looked up with a look of discovery on her face, "I didn't realize this before but that's probably how I got the idea that I was somehow helping my mother if I succeeded at school. Silly what little kids will think. I felt so bad for my mother, alone and working so hard. I just loved bringing home my report card with all those A's. Her face would beam with pride. I guess I was trying to make up for Dad being gone."

Elizabeth described her early school years. "I've always liked school. I know how influential a teacher can be. That's probably why I'm in education today. I felt more at home at school than I did in that large, empty house. As soon as I got home each afternoon I would wish it was tomorrow already so I could go back to school. Since I worked so hard, I was usually ahead of the class. My third-grade teacher even let me lead a special tutoring group all by myself. She led one group and I led the other. Was I ever thrilled!"

Trouble came for Elizabeth, however, in her fourth-grade year when she was placed in a class with a rigidly structured teacher who demanded that Elizabeth work at the same pace as the rest of the class. If she finished early, Elizabeth was forced to sit in her seat and wait for the others. "It is a bit embarrassing to admit this," Elizabeth glanced at me out of the corner of her green eyes with a sheepish grin, "but I really gave that poor lady a hard time. I used all my energy coming up with ways to upset her without getting caught. One day I convinced one of the boys to tape a sign to her back that said, 'Kick me.' I felt so smug. She walked around with that sign all afternoon. She came up to me shaking with anger and said, 'I know you are behind this, and, believe me, I'm going to catch you yet!' But she never did."

"I just hated school that year. My grades dropped. It was the first time I had made a B. I felt like a failure. I begged my mother to take me out of that place." Even though it placed an additional financial burden on their limited resources, Elizabeth convinced her mother to place her in a private school. "Dad had reappeared by this time and was giving us some money from time to time. Things were still tight, however, and my mom said, 'If you go to that private school, I won't have money to buy you new clothes or take you out places.' I told her I didn't care—just get me out of that class."

The new school became Elizabeth's haven through her high school years. She was active in the math club, president of the debate team, and editor of the school newspaper.

"What about dating or close friends?" I inquired. Elizabeth shrugged her shoulders with an indifferent air. "The boys all seemed so immature, and I was busy with my projects so I didn't feel the need for many friends. The only person I really talked to back then was my mom. We were like best friends. She would talk about the men she was dating and ask my advice. That made me feel important."

Elizabeth paused for a moment, and a wave of sadness flooded her face. "Looking back now, I do remember once when I felt lonely, even odd. I worked on the yearbook when I was a senior. The yearbook staff was so excited when the books came in. As usual, I asked to help the teacher, and he let me distribute the books. Everyone grabbed their copy and began running around getting people to sign their books. I just stood there. You know, not one student asked me to sign their book. The teacher noticed and asked me to sign his. He was the only person who signed my senior yearbook, and I can still remember what he wrote: 'To an exceptionally talented young woman. I hope you accomplish all your dreams.' "

The Messiah Trap was set for Elizabeth when, as a child, Elizabeth learned to "help" her mother by overachieving in school and to help her teachers by tutoring her peers. As an adolescent, Elizabeth was unable to relate to students her own age and instead claimed her mother as her "best friend." All these experiences put Elizabeth into adult caregiving roles prematurely.

In addition to being placed in an adult role prematurely, Elizabeth experienced childhood trauma that had been inadequately resolved. While divorce is difficult for all children, the divorce of

Elizabeth's parents was especially damaging. First of all, Elizabeth's father did not continue any form of contact with her during her younger years. This abandonment marked Elizabeth deeply, so deeply that she pretended it didn't hurt. Elizabeth did not refer to him very often.

At the same time, Elizabeth's mother was forced to go to work. This second loss cut deep into her young heart. Elizabeth again tried to ignore this loss by refusing to remember watching her mother leave her each day at the school. But two-year-old Elizabeth knew that Daddy had left her and not reappeared.

What guarantee did she have that her mother would not do the same? The trauma Elizabeth experienced day after day caused her to doubt her own worth. She began to feel different from the other children because she came from a "broken" home. Elizabeth tried to find a way to fix her broken home and her broken heart.

Because of the unresolved pain in her childhood, Elizabeth became a "helpaholic." She developed the eight characteristics evident in most Messiahs. The Messiah is one who

1. Tries to earn a sense of worth by "acting" worthy
2. Lets others determine his or her actions
3. Needs to overachieve
4. Is attracted to helping those with similar pain
5. Experiences difficulty in establishing peer and intimate relationships
6. Is caught in a cycle of isolation
7. Is driven to endless activity
8. Stops when he or she drops

1. TRIES TO EARN A SENSE OF WORTH BY "ACTING" WORTHY

> As a child, Elizabeth often stayed after class to clean erasers for her favorite teachers. Now she worked late processing funding proposals for the motivated teachers on her staff.

Although Messiahs may pretend to feel important, underneath the surface Messiahs often doubt their value. In an effort to earn a sense of worth, Messiahs are motivated to accomplish "worthwhile" goals. They transfer attention from developing an *inner* sense of specialness to *external* achievement. They try to excel in such a way as to gain a desired response from those they view as worthwhile—usually parents, teachers, or other authority figures. As children, Messiahs develop skills that are valued by adults, which most often include being "helpful" to those adults on whom the child Messiahs depend.

In school, Elizabeth was indirectly taught that she could earn her worth by meeting the expectations of the teachers. She realized that it was the teachers, not the students, who gave out the grades. Consequently, she neglected her need for friends. What mattered to Elizabeth was praise and acceptance from the adults who promised to stay in her life—at least for as long as the school year lasted.

When placed in a classroom where the teacher did not reward her overachievement, she became despondent and depressed. Elizabeth swung to the other extreme and traded her extra-good behavior for extra-bad behavior. One way or the other, Elizabeth had to stand out in the crowd. If she were just another child in the room, Elizabeth was afraid that she, like her father, might disappear.

Like Elizabeth, Messiahs are adults who were once children, dependent on adults for the meeting of physical and emotional needs. Since most Messiahs grew up believing that good behavior would be rewarded and misbehavior would be punished, pleasing these adults seemed equivalent to securing survival. When in danger or emotionally neglected or abused, Messiah children tend to assume they are being punished because they have been "bad" children. Efforts, then, are focused on being good, which is defined as acting in accordance to the wishes of adults.

Messiah children are usually taught that good people always do good things and say good things. Good people never say mean things. They don't even have mean thoughts. Good people don't get angry and are always cheerful, especially through hardship. Most of all, good people are always thinking of others and they are never, ever selfish. Messiah children are often told things like "Don't say that. That's not nice. Good children don't say things like that." That well-worn phrase can be used by adults when children express any feeling that causes adults distress or discomfort.

As a result, Messiahs learn that certain feelings are unacceptable. Messiah children are not only forbidden to express certain feelings, but *they are not to feel these feelings at all.* Consequently, many Messiahs learn to cut off from their emotions, unable as adults to feel parts of their inner selves.

2. LETS OTHERS DETERMINE HIS OR HER ACTIONS

> Elizabeth insisted on an "open door" policy for her office. Whenever a student or teacher needed her, she was available, even when it meant she had to work on Saturdays to meet her own deadlines.

Since the Messiah depends on the response of others for a sense of well-being, it is common for the Messiah allow his or her actions to be determined by others. Messiahs need the approval from others to feel special and so will behave according to others' dictates. It is very important to recognize that, when you are caught in the Messiah Trap, you give up control over your own life and over your own sense of well-being.

Because Messiahs are so busy trying to please others, personal interests are seldom cultivated. What would you like to do if you weren't trapped into taking care of others? Do you *really* know? Most Messiahs haven't a clue. In the desperate search for self-esteem, most Messiahs listen to others, not to themselves. Messiahs become involved in activities that will provide positive feedback from others. Often neglected are those activities that may not be valued by other people but that may address the Messiah's needs and desires. These include the development of peer relationships, personal nurturance skills, and taking time to explore the spiritual realm.

3. NEEDS TO OVERACHIEVE

> Elizabeth always kept her desk cleared of papers and clutter. She never missed a deadline and always came to meetings prepared.

Messiahs, in the attempt to earn a sense of value, tend to overachieve and overperform. Elizabeth was content only when "succeeding" in school. But how did Elizabeth define success? She needed to achieve a straight-A report card in order to feel acceptable. This is very important to note. While having straight A's is not required by all Messiahs, most are perfectionists in some specific area.

In order to feel *acceptable* to others, Messiahs are often enslaved to the pursuit of proving themselves *indispensable* to others in order to feel acceptable. To achieve the status of special, the Messiah tries to run faster, jump higher, advance quicker than others. In response to the Messiah's devotion to overachievement, others may call them "superstars," "exceptionally talented," or "achieving well beyond his or her years." If the Messiah doesn't *over*achieve, but achieves on an age-appropriate level, at pace with natural abilities, he or she often feels like a failure. Messiahs have to be *better* to feel *worthwhile* at all.

4. IS ATTRACTED TO HELPING THOSE WITH SIMILAR PAIN

> Elizabeth developed a special program for mentally gifted children in her school and diligently worked to obtain scholarship money for students from low-income and single-parent homes.

Rather than deal with her needs and pain directly, Elizabeth became involved in meeting the needs and addressing the pain in other people's lives. Like Elizabeth, Messiahs are naturally and unconsciously attracted to other people who share a common childhood pain. Elizabeth devoted her adult years to helping youngsters who reminded her of herself when she was a child. She was drawn to others, compelled to help, because she so desperately needed help herself.

Stop for a moment and think back on those people you have helped recently. Do you help everyone that comes into your path? Probably not. You most likely help certain types of people. I have friends and clients who are especially sensitive to the needs of the elderly, some to particular family members, others to the homeless. I have a soft spot in my heart for children. It is not uncommon for victims of sexual abuse to become therapists who specialize in treating victims of molestation, for children of alcoholic parents to write books on alcoholism, or for children of divorced parents to become attorneys specializing in family law. When caught in the Messiah Trap, you may be driven to help others because you are so woefully neglecting yourself.

5. EXPERIENCES DIFFICULTY IN ESTABLISHING PEER AND INTIMATE RELATIONSHIPS

> Elizabeth met another single principal in her late twenties from the local public junior high at a conference. The next week Elizabeth picked up the phone to invite her to go shopping, but each time she hung up before the other woman answered. She convinced herself that her own lower salary would make it hard to enjoy shopping at the best stores.

A well-balanced individual will be able to comfortably perform in three capacities. There will be a time to lead (superior to subordinate), a time to follow (subordinate to superior), and a time to walk beside someone else (peer to peer). The Messiah, however, is limited in his or her capacity to relate to others. Deep inside most Messiahs is a little child who feels powerless to protect him or herself. This frightening feeling is masked by taking on the most powerful role available—that of helper (superior to subordinate).

When we help someone, we are in the superior role while the person receiving our help is in the subordinate role. The helper has more power, more prestige, and is often considered an "expert." The person receiving help, on the other hand, is considered needy and dependent on the helper. While many Messiahs claim to be "serving" others, they are nevertheless playing the most powerful role.

Playing the powerful role of helper may not seem too crucial to the Messiah—that is, until it is taken away. Then it becomes apparent just how much that power is needed. Think about yourself for a moment. How well do you receive assistance from others? How often do you ask for help? I have observed many people who have fallen into the Messiah Trap who are hurting and needy and overwhelmed—but who cannot seem to accept help. Most Messiahs have great difficulty receiving gifts, letting people throw parties in their honor, or calling a friend when their car breaks down on the highway. Messiahs don't mind giving people rides or dropping off bags of groceries to shut-ins but will writhe in frustration and even humiliation should they need transportation or need to call a friend to drop by some food when ill.

Occasionally Messiahs are able to accept the role of subordinate, but only in clearly defined situations. These include more formal relationships, such as employee to employer, or parishioner to pastor. Elizabeth felt comfortable playing the role of student. She had the most difficulty, however, when asked to relate peer to peer.

Many Messiahs may look as if they have peer relationships. Not all Messiahs are as isolated as Elizabeth. Some are quite outgoing and have a wide circle of "friends." But on close inspection, it becomes evident that the Messiah has difficulty in relating on equal footing with these so-called peers. Instead of developing relationships with peers as equals, Messiahs tend to use peers as points of competition, as standards against which to measure a sense of specialness. Elizabeth saw herself as important when she was selected to lead the reading group. She had succeeded in achieving a special status, that of the helper role. She—unknowingly—also separated herself from her peers. In her success, Elizabeth sacrificed an important opportunity to develop friendships with her classmates. Instead she identified herself with the teacher and thereby took on a pseudo-adult role.

It is my observation that Messiahs try to avoid situations wherein they are expected to be one of the group. Messiahs most often avoid peer relationships and social gatherings by giving the great Messiah excuse, "I would really like to come but I'm just too busy." If unable to avoid the situation, Messiahs may try to move into roles of leadership (disguised as helping): "Sure, I'll come. What can I do to help? Want me to arrange the transportation? (bring a video, organize the refreshments, come early and decorate?)"

Should the Messiah fail to avoid the situation or gain control by helping, effort is usually made in channeling the conversation to nonpersonal issues. "Have you read that new book by so-and-so?" "Can you believe the amount of violence on TV today?" "How do you feel we should address the issue of world hunger?" If personal issues are discussed, you can be certain they will be *someone else's* personal problems, which the Messiah is more than willing to try to solve.

Most Messiahs do not relate easily to others as peers and rarely disclose personal, especially problematic, information. As children, Messiahs were unable to acquire the skills necessary for the development of peer relationships, which lay the groundwork for the development of intimate relationships as adults. When robbed of this opportunity, Messiahs inevitably have difficulty in adult intimate relationships. Messiahs, like Elizabeth, pay a high price to be special by ending up being separated from the group and missing out on acquiring fundamental relationship skills.

6. IS CAUGHT IN A CYCLE OF ISOLATION

> At that same conference, Elizabeth busied herself by browsing at the book tables as the meetings broke for lunch. She hoped no one would notice she was alone, yet she couldn't bear the idea of joining the special lunch table set aside for newcomers. She slipped out and ate alone at a nearby deli.

Messiahs tend to experience a deep sense of isolation. While in the presence of other people, the Messiah may feel excruciatingly lonely. This is due, in part, to the fact that *the Messiah cannot be a part of the group and feel special at the same time.* Elizabeth was driven by the emptiness and pain inside of her to be seen as better. But better turned out to be "different." When she felt different, she also felt odd and this underscored her feelings of inferiority.

Elizabeth was caught in the Messiah cycle—feelings of worthlessness propelled her toward attempting to be special. She tried to be special by being different, but being different left her feeling isolated and odd. This intensified her feelings of worthlessness, which once again propelled her toward proving her specialness—and the cycle continued.

Elizabeth found herself, at the end of her high school days, feeling alone in a room of peers. Her only human connection was with a teacher who pitied her. The message he wrote in her yearbook summed up the lie she had been taught so well—that she could "accomplish" her dreams by being "exceptional." The truth of the matter is that Elizabeth will never be able to experience the wholeness of life as long as she tries to *achieve* a feeling of worth through pleasing others and isolating herself from her peers.

7. IS DRIVEN TO ENDLESS ACTIVITY

> Elizabeth worked every Saturday. People soon stopped calling her for social activities, knowing she would answer, "I've got too much to do."

Messiahs do a great deal of pretending—pretending they were not hurt as children, pretending they do not feel worthless and powerless. This pretense is maintained by doing things other people consider worthwhile and by taking on powerful roles, hoping that no one will find out about the pain inside.

Since we are trying to establish a sense of worth through external achievement, the Messiah cannot rest. The Messiah becomes addicted to helping. Successes achieved are not internalized so they are not trusted. Regardless of the college degrees earned, the professional status attained, and the noble sacrifices made, Messiahs still *feel* worthless. Any sense of self-regard that may be gleaned from these positive experiences is often short-lived, if enjoyed at all. Consequently, Messiahs must keep on achieving.

During periods of inactivity, Messiahs usually experience many uncomfortable feelings such as guilt, depression, and/or anxiety. Messiahs often feel guilty if they are not out helping someone in need or achieving something measurable.

Anxiety creeps in with the fear of being seen as selfish or useless. The Messiah may feel depressed but not know why. As a young student, Elizabeth became despondent when she was expected to sit quietly in her chair and wait. Waiting is a form of torture for most Messiahs. A restlessness is generated by the inner sense of inferiorty that pushes Messiahs into an endless search for activity. And so the Messiah helps and helps and helps.

Do you want to know how ensnared you are by the Messiah Trap? Ask yourself these questions: How did you feel the last time someone teased you about taking it easy or loafing around? Did you defend yourself by listing all you had accomplished that day? If you have an evening free, do you feel guilty about spending that time on yourself? Or do you find something "useful" to do—useful to someone else? Do you find it necessary to justify taking a vacation? Or do you never take a vacation because you can never find the time? Since Messiahs have to reach perfection just to feel that they have broken even, Messiahs become quite agitated if accused of "taking it easy" or "loafing around." Messiahs overreact to such terms because to Messiahs they translate into "worthless" and "unacceptable." To someone else, these terms may just describe your current good fortune of some leisure time. But not to Messiahs, not to those who are fighting to justify their very existence.

8. STOPS WHEN HE OR SHE DROPS

> Elizabeth's work week extended to nearly sixty hours. Two nights a week she met with the board of the local community college. On Sundays at church, she coordinated the church school program.

Messiahs inevitably take on much more than can be humanly accomplished. I have heard many Messiahs complain that there are too few hours in a day, which means they have taken on more than they can handle. Messiahs are frantically trying to outrun their human limitations. Messiahs would very much enjoy being gods with unlimited capabilities. Why? Because then maybe enough could be accomplished to earn peace of mind, a sense of value, the right to be loved.

Most Messiahs continue this race toward the elusive sense of well-being until they drop. I've watched Messiahs collapse from fatigue, develop debilitating illnesses, or drown in depression. Messiahs have chosen to allow their marriages to disintegrate, their careers to spin out of control, and their children to suffer emotional neglect rather than give up the race. Withdrawing from the race is usually considered defeat and so, rather than be "defeated," Messiahs will watch their lives crumble and try to call that *noble*.

A few Messiahs, very few unfortunately, begin to question why they are running at all. Elizabeth came to counseling because she had grown weary of this race. She suspected the truth: this Messiah race *cannot* be won, simply because this Messiah race is a *trap*. Overachievement had not made Elizabeth happy as promised. Helping others feel better about themselves had not satisfied the hunger inside herself, and she wanted to know why. Although Elizabeth did not realize it at the time, she was taking the first step on a new and exciting journey. She was no longer willing to pretend, and was gathering up the courage to finally face the pain of her childhood.

5. What Kind of Messiah Are You?

The Messiah Quiz

1. Do you spend your time at social gatherings making sure everyone is having a good time? Are you a Pleaser?
2. Was your evening at home again interrupted by the call of a friend in crisis, and you dropped everything to run out and help? Are you a Rescuer?
3. Did you agree to help a friend move on your only free Saturday this month? Are you a Giver?
4. Were you up late again last night listening to someone struggle with his or her problems but, this morning, could think of no one you felt could listen to yours? Are you a Counselor?
5. Did you try to help a couple of friends work out their differences, got caught in the middle, and they both turned on you? Are you a Protector?
6. Are you overwhelmed by the number of groups you are leading, presentations you are making, and study or preparation that has to be done? Are you a Teacher?
7. Do you find yourself so driven to fight for a worthy cause that, between the committee meetings, newsletters, and fundraisers, you are about to drop from exhaustion? Are you a Crusader?

Anyone can fall into the Messiah Trap. It is an equal opportunity entrapper. Men as well as women, rich as well as poor, strong as well as weak have fallen prey to the Messiah Trap.

While all Messiahs to some extent believe the lies of the Messiah Trap, each lives out these lies in different ways. There are probably as many kinds of Messiahs as there are Messiahs. I have identified at least seven different styles Messiahs tend to take on:

1. Pleaser
2. Rescuer
3. Giver
4. Counselor
5. Protector
6. Teacher
7. Crusader

A Messiah can display characteristics of one, several, or all seven. The following Messiahs may help you better identify which style or styles may describe you.

THE PLEASER

In one of our initial sessions, Elizabeth was asked to describe her work week. The energy seemed to drain out of her, her shoulders slumped, and a darkness spread across her face. "There's always more to do than there is time. This week it's a new fundraising campaign for the school. I just couldn't say 'no'. It's such a worthy cause, and no one else on the board has had the right experience. Besides, everyone else is already serving on two or three subcommittees. And I thought to myself, 'Someone has to do it.' "

Elizabeth spread open her multicolored, multisectioned day planner on her lap to show the week's calendar. "Look at this!" Elizabeth gasped in desperation. "I have every fifteen-minute slot filled for the entire week! There is just no way that I'll be able to do all the things I've agreed to do." She paused and frowned at her feet for a moment. When she looked up at me again, there was a deep sadness in her eyes. "I hate letting these people down. It just kills me."

"How have you been taking care of yourself lately?" I asked her. Elizabeth closed her calendar and pushed it aside. "Taking care of myself? You've got to be kidding. Who's got the time? I've been driving through fast food spots as I dash from meeting to meeting. Sleep? I think I've forgotten how! My mother called the other night and left a message on my answering machine asking if she could have an appointment with me. Can you believe that? An 'appointment'! I felt so guilty!"

The competent woman Elizabeth tried to project to the world seemed to shrink meekly into the cushions. "I'm so tired. I don't know how much longer I can keep this up. I just can't seem to keep everyone happy at the same time."

There was silence in the room. "Are *you* happy?" I asked. Her tired eyes filled with tears. "No, I'm not happy. I'm miserable."

Pleasers like Elizabeth try to make other people happy. Pleasers tend to be very conscientious and caring people. Being especially sensitive to other people's feelings, Pleasers can often read the emotions of others with alarming accuracy. It is common for these Messiahs to go out of their way to make others feel comfortable and may put a great deal of energy into doing "little things" for other people.

Desiring to be sensitive and responsive to the needs of others is a valuable quality without which our relationships would become battlefields rather than places of refuge and nurturance. There is hopefully a little pleaser in each of us. The Messiah Pleaser, however, is someone who begins with a desire to please but then translates this desire into a responsibility. Pleasers feel *responsible* for other people's happiness, and when others are displeased Pleasers usually experience feelings of guilt and failure.

Since Pleasers take on the unrealistic responsibility for the well-being of others, they will almost always agree to do whatever is asked, whether there is time or not. And, because Pleasers always say "yes," more and more people soon arrive with requests. Pleasers are asked to serve on just one more committee, coach one more basketball team, teach that difficult Sunday School class or make a quick run by the cleaners to pick up the gray suit by 4 P.M. It is the Pleaser in us that gets us to bite our lip rather than say, "No, it really is an imposition to have that report ready by tomorrow." Pleasers choose to suffer rather than disappoint anyone else.

While some Pleasers become overextended in a variety of obligations, others become overinvested in one person, situation, or project. A minister's wife may become overinvested in church work, thereby neglecting her family and personal growth. A therapist may become overly attached to a particular needy or talented client, to the neglect of others in the client load. A son or daughter may be drawn into the parents' marital difficulties, thereby investing time and energy into supplementing an inadequate marriage. As a result of this overinvestment, the child is robbed of the legitimate opportunity to invest in his or her own personal relationships. Pleasers who become overinvested in the lives of others may feel overwhelmed by the magnitude of the problems, yet feel trapped by a sense of responsibility.

I have identified two types of pleasers—the Organizing Pleaser and the Spontaneous Pleaser. Elizabeth is a perfect example of the first category. Organizing Pleasers do just that—organize people, events, and situations in order to please others. Other examples of Organizing Pleasers include program directors who pull together wilderness programs for inner-city youth, board members who help social service agencies, or wedding coordinators who straighten out everything from the ushers' boutonnieres to the clean-up crew after the reception.

Not only do Organizing Pleasers organize others, they also organize themselves. Pleasers say "yes" with every intention of following through but very soon have too many tasks to perform and too many people expecting assistance. In response to this unrealistic load, most Pleasers try to pedal faster, sleep less, and do more. Organizing Pleasers respond to this enormous workload by getting even more "organized." Like Elizabeth, Organizing Pleasers often get specially designed notebooks with color-coded organizer sheets to streamline their lives and produce more. They grab meals by driving through the local fast food restaurant. They schedule prayer and meditation time into the moments spent bumper-to-bumper on the freeway, headed for the next meeting.

While Organizing Pleasers are structured and make plans months in advance, Spontaneous Pleasers simplify this dilemma by trying to please whomever they are with at any given time. Spontaneous Pleasers tend to take life as it comes and take people life seems to bring their way. This is not to imply that Spontaneous Pleasers take pleasing others any less seriously than Organizing Pleasers. Pleasing is very serious business for all Pleasers. Spontaneous Pleasers simply have a different style. The present moment is what matters, and the person who is currently presenting a need takes priority over all previous obligations.

Since Spontaneous Pleasers tend to say "yes" to every person encountered, agreements made with one person often conflict with other arrangements made. Multiple agreements can result in extremely complex and chaotic situations. This can be especially damaging when the Spontaneous Pleaser is the head of a group or organization because the Spontaneous Pleaser says "yes" to everyone's request. It can appear that the Spontaneous Pleaser is lying, but this is not the case. The need to please is so great that Spontaneous Pleasers feel compelled to help everyone and may experience intense agony if forced to make a decision wherein someone is denied his or her request.

All Pleasers, whether organized or spontaneous, have difficulty in expressing personal feelings should those feelings be unpopular or potentially unpleasing to someone else. Pleasers will swallow anger, hide fatigue, or disguise depression rather than let someone else down. I've watched Pleasers endure migraine headaches rather than express their rage, suffer from repeated bouts with viruses rather than take time off, or develop ulcers rather than delegate responsibilities.

Like Elizabeth, Pleasers begin with a desire to please but soon become addicted to pleasing by attempting the impossible—taking responsibility for other people's happiness (Side 1: "If I don't do it, it won't get done.") By saying "yes" when he or she wants to say "no", the Pleaser ends up with too many duties and far too much pain (Side 2: "Everyone else's needs take priority over mine"). Pleasers dance to someone else's tune with feet tangled in frustration and in their denial of true feelings.

THE RESCUER

"Everyone in the whole world is mad at me," said Dale in despair as he flopped his long, thin frame onto the couch. Even though he adjusted his tie that had flipped over his shoulder and tried to smooth the wrinkles from his tailored pants, he was still unable to achieve a balanced appearance. "I'll bet you're even mad at me!" When asked what cause I would have to be angry, he aimed his deep blue eyes at me. "Well, I'm late again, aren't I?" he challenged. "Go ahead. Tell me how I've let you down like all the rest."

"Do you feel you've let people down recently?" I asked.

"I've tried not to. No one seems to appreciate what I do for them. Take today, for example. Some of the guys at work play in a tournament and were complaining that, since one of the players was out sick, they would have to forfeit the game. I said I would be glad to fill in tonight after work, and they were thrilled.

"But as I was leaving for the game, one of my clients called, a young mother I'm representing in a custody case, crying hysterically over a letter she had received from her ex-husband. She was really upset. I told her I couldn't talk now, but she really started falling apart. So I drove over to her place to help her sort all this out."

"By the time she calmed down and I got over to the gym, the game had been forfeited. Some of the guys were walking out. 'Thanks a lot, Dale. Sure glad we can count on you,' one of them said. When I tried to explain, he just waved me away with his hand and said, 'I never have any trouble both dealing with my clients *and* keeping my word. You're always 'rescuing' someone, Dale.' The guy next to him snarled under his breath, 'Too bad he couldn't have rescued us instead of some damsel in distress.' They all laughed at me and left.

"Sometimes it *does* feel like I go from crisis to crisis." Dale rested his head in the palms of his large hands. "I'm just trying to help. It's backfiring on me somehow. I just don't understand it."

In the same way that Pleasers attract people with requests, Rescuers attract people in crisis. Like Dale, Rescuers may become overinvested in one or two people who seem to go from crisis to crisis, trauma to trauma. Rescuers tend to drop everything to aid someone in trouble, regardless of the personal hardship it may cause them or even cause to others who expect assistance. Consequently, the Rescuer may be considered unreliable by those left behind as the Rescuer runs off to the rescue.

Besides sacrificing a reputation for being reliable, Rescuers also sacrifice privacy and the ability to plan ahead. Rescuers are always "on call" for unexpected crises and may live in continual dread of the ring of the phone or the knock on the door.

Like all Rescuers, Dale fell into the Messiah Trap when he saw himself as the only one who could help (Side 1: "If I don't do it, it won't get done") and that, since it was a "crisis," all other needs or obligations were ignored (Side 2: "Everyone else's needs take priority over mine"). He was caught in the Trap, addicted to rescuing, when assisting someone in crisis ceased to be an occasional activity, triggered by life's inevitable tragedies, and instead became a way of life. Rescuers turn rescuing into a lifestyle.

THE GIVER

The tight brunette curls bobbed up and down as Alicia silently sobbed into her tiny hands. After several minutes, she raised her tear-streaked face and began talking about her three children. "It's so hard trying to raise them alone. There always seem to be twice as many bills and half as much money as I need." She reached for a tissue, dabbed her large brown eyes, and continued, "It really hurts me when my kids ask for things that their friends have and I don't have the money."

Waving the tissue in the air, her face tightened up in frustration. "And besides the kids there are so many other responsibilities. My sister, for example. Tanya keeps showing up at my door at dinner time expecting to eat. I do want her to feel welcome, don't get me wrong. We're family, after all. I just don't know how to tell her I can't afford to feed her all the time. I just couldn't ask her for money."

"I'll tell you what really breaks my heart are those starving children I saw on a TV special the other night. I sat there thinking, 'How can you complain, Alicia? Look at all you've got!' A friend of mine had just sent me a check for my birthday. She wanted me to get some new clothes. It's been so long since I've gone shopping for myself." She looked across the room as if looking back in time. "It must have been before Richard left me." Turning her round face back toward me, Alicia resumed her story. "But I felt so bad for those little children that I wrote a check for the amount of my present and put it right in the mail." She shrugged those slim shoulders that seem to carry the burdens of the world. "How could I feel happy about buying a dress when those little ones are dying?" She looked me straight in the eye. "How?"

Givers, like Alicia, tend to be generous people who delight in the act of giving. One of the Giver's greatest thrills is to watch someone receive a gift, to see the joy spread across his or her face. It is especially exciting when the Giver is able to provide something that the receiver would otherwise go without.

When Givers hear of the deprivation that exists in this world, the Giver's response is often one of guilt and a sense of personal responsibility for meeting those needs (Side 1: "If I don't do it, it won't get done"). Many of us have enjoyed so much bounty in this country that to withhold anything for ourselves seems to border on immorality (Side 2: "Everyone else's needs take priority over mine"). As in Alicia's situation, Givers fall into the Messiah Trap when the *opportunity* to give is viewed as an *obligation*. If a person has no choice but to give, he or she is no longer giving but are being taken. When a person feels taken, the joy is replaced by resentment. Since Messiah Givers are addicted to giving and therefore unable to place realistic limits on giving, the tendency is to give and give and give, and stop only when there is nothing left but feelings of guilt and fatigue.

THE COUNSELOR

"Did you enjoy your sister's wedding?" I asked as the session began. Diedre pulled her sweater more tightly around herself. "I don't know how I get myself into these things."

Folding her arms, Diedre assured me, "The wedding itself went fine. Andrea and Frank make a fine couple. I've always worried about Andrea, being the baby of the family and all. But it looks like she may have finally found a man who will put up with her demands." Diedre paused. "At the reception, well, you know how I seem to have a knack for picking up poor souls in trouble. There was this forlorn-looking woman—attractive, actually—hanging out at the punch bowl. She seemed alone and awkward, so I went over to be friendly."

Diedre flashed a full smile at me. "You know who she was? My new brother-in-law's ex-girlfriend! Heartbroken, to be sure." Diedre's smile faded. "Quite a sad situation actually. When Andrea and Frank came in to the reception, I could see that she was about to cry, so I took her outside for a walk." Her frown deepened. "She sobbed and sobbed, so I stayed with her and helped her as best I could. We must have talked for two hours! By the time I got back into the building, almost everyone had left."

"I missed getting to see my sister before she left for her honeymoon. My mother was angry at me because they couldn't find me for the family pictures. Of couse, my husband was furious because he said I left him alone again while I took care of someone else." She shrugged her shoulders. "But what could I do? Abandon this poor creature? I couldn't. She needed me."

Counselors such as Diedre are empathic people drawn to those who are confused by a problem situation. With the help of the Counselor, old problems are often seen from new perspectives. Having a natural curiosity and talent for understanding the complex human condition, Counselors have a special knack for getting people to open up their secrets and their pain. Multitudes of people crave to be heard, but there are very few listeners. Counselors listen—so people talk.

Having a need to counsel, Counselors have a proclivity to recruit people who need someone to listen to them. Diedre, like many Counselors, rarely waited until someone sought her out. It was easy for Diedre to spot people in distress, and so she was soon pulling them aside for private conversations. Since Counselors do not take well to small talk, they move the conversation with relative ease from the weather to whether or not the marriage will last or what triggered that last bout of depression. Not willing to accept polite comments of "Oh, I'm fine, thanks," Counselors prefer to ask, "How are you doing *really?*"

Having become helpaholics, Counselors find themselves counseling in a majority, if not all, interactions with others—with hairdressers and tailors, secretaries and bosses. Very often Counselors turn dates into counseling sessions and business lunches into group therapy. Offering a listening ear, Counselors counsel parents, lovers, and friends. However, by turning every social situation into an opportunity to counsel, Counselors are often robbed of needed time for relaxation and renewal.

Another problem Counselors face is the potential of becoming overwhelmed by other people's problems. When listening as others describe and unload their pain, their problem is then shared by both parties. This is one reason why counseling is so effective—two people come together and share the load. Counselors may take in more pain, however, than can be easily managed. In one day a Counselor can experience the horror of molestation, the grief of divorce, and the despair of depression. Experiencing other people's trauma can become overwhelming.

By getting so caught up in the struggles of other people, Counselors may lose sight of the reality that they too have problems to face. I have known Counselors who successfully help their clients express feelings and yet are unable to even identify feelings they themselves may have. Counselors may spend nights in sleepless worry over the problems of others but do not attend to their own troubles. Some are afraid to explore those dark regions where feelings lurk, finding it much easier to tell young married couples how to express their feelings of tenderness than to tell their own spouses of their own deep loneliness. While helping adolescents express their rage to their parents, Counselors may brush off their own anger with a cool, 'Oh, everything is just fine . . . " Once in the Messiah Trap, Counselors make better "travel agents" than "tour guides": it is easy to hand out maps and set up the itinerary, but Messiah Counselors don't really know the territory, because they have yet to explore their own dark, inner regions.

Another dilemma that often faces the Counselor is finding someone in which to confide. Counselors are looked up to as people with answers—and are certainly not supposed to be people with problems. Consequently, it may be difficult to find a place where the Counselor can be honest about inner struggles. Where does the pastor go to grapple with the affair he is having? Whom does the social worker confide in when she loses control and batters her child? Where do we go with our own inner pain? Like Diedre, many Counselors do not take the risk of such exposure, and continue to hide from life in the feelings of others.

THE PROTECTOR

Cindi and Paul sat at opposite ends of the couch, radiating opposing emotions. Everything about Cindi was cross—her legs were crossed, her arms were folded firmly across her. She had twisted her body so that only her back was visible to her husband. Paul seemed to feel this disapproval most acutely, as his hands moved anxiously in his lap. His head was bowed but tilted slightly to keep a woeful eye on his wife, in the hope of some sign of reprieve.

In an explosive rush Cindi barked, "Do you know what he did?" She nodded the back of her head, pointing to her husband. "He hid my mail from me for three months! Three *months!*"

"I was just trying to help." Paul insisted in defense.

"Help?" Cindi swung around to face her trembling husband. "How can you call stealing my mail *help?*" Before Paul could speak, she turned to me. "I was working on the final draft of my dissertation yesterday afternoon and began sorting through one of our closets looking for a book I needed for the bibliography.

Know what I found buried in the closet?" She glared at Paul. "Three months of mail. My MAIL! There were personal letters, wedding announcements, party invitations. I couldn't believe it. I'd wondered why certain friends weren't calling anymore. They're probably wondering why I've been ignoring them! Here I am married to a pastor, whom I thought I could trust, and now I find that he has stolen my mail! I am so hurt and angry."

The silence seemed to point its finger at Paul, "I was just trying to protect you, Cindi. I knew how important this doctorate was to you, and people are always making such demands on your time." Paul looked pleadingly at me. "You know how overwhelmed she can get. I was going to give her all that mail once she finished. I never thought she would be angry."

He smiled embarrassedly. "You know what I expected? I had this whole fantasy about the day she would finish her dissertation. I would bring out the mail, and she would throw her arms around me in gratitude." Even though his voice was low I could see his anger rising. "I thought she'd be grateful for how I protected her from herself."

It was Paul's turn to cross his arms and turn his back to his wife. To the wall he muttered, "I'm sick and tired of trying so hard to help and being unappreciated. Sick and tired!"

Protectors, like Paul, are caring people who overstep the bounds of the possible. By taking on the responsibility of protecting others, Protectors assume a responsibility that is beyond human capability. One way the Messiah tries to protect others is by keeping secret potentially harmful information in much the same way that Paul tried to protect Cindi from "herself" by hiding her mail.

Another way Protectors overstep their boundaries is by passing on too much information. Protectors may overhear private conversations, pick up bits of news in staff meetings, observe interactions in social gatherings—all of which provide information that may be considered helpful to someone else. So the Protector passes it along. This may even mean breaking promises or confidentiality. As a consequence, efforts at protection may be misunderstood and seen as intrusive or dishonest.

Protectors often feel responsible for making choices for others in their behalf. (Side 1: "If I don't do it, it won't get done.") At times, Protectors go to great lengths to protect others (Side 2: "Everyone else's needs take priority over mine.") However, as Paul found out, the sacrifices of the Protector may be great but the appreciation scarce.

THE TEACHER

The first time I saw Gary, he was enthusiastically debating some issue at a conference we were attending. His eyes were full of life and good humor, excited about the issues, charged by the controversy. Now he was sitting anxiously on my couch, lacing and unlacing his fingers. The sparkle was gone. His eyes were dull, red-rimmed, and puffy. When I urged him to tell me why he had asked for a session, he sighed and began to explain his history.

"When I arrived at graduate school, I thought the whole world was out there for me. Everything went perfectly. My master teacher and I hit it off immediately. He offered me a teaching assistant position, which is almost unheard of for a first-year student. Soon he allowed me to deliver some of my own lectures. The next thing I knew I was being asked to speak at retreats, conferences, youth rallies. After graduate school, my career just took off." Gary smiled for the first time. "I loved it."

"Then it just got out of hand, somehow. I couldn't seem to turn down any speaking requests. In addition to my full teaching load, I started leading a weekly group on campus. I became a regular presenter at the community forum in town. I don't mean to sound bragadocious, but it seems like everyone wants me to speak. I have a speaking engagement or retreat scheduled every weekend until Christmas."

He pulled himself in, sat upright, and began to pick at a thread in one of the couch pillows. "My home life is nearly nonexistent. Annie, my wife, is always complaining about my never being home. She told me the other night that my kids are growing up without a father. It's true. My oldest just graduated from high school. Where has the time gone?"

"When I'm not in class, I'm on my way to a presentation. When I'm not speaking, I'm preparing for the next week's retreat. It's a never-ending treadmill. Sometimes I don't even remember which crowd I'm addressing."

"It's ironic. Here I spend all my time telling other people how to get the most out of life and their relationships, and I don't seem to have any life of my own at all. I don't know what to do."

Teachers, like Gary, are unique from other types of Messiahs in that Teachers try to help people by the group load. Examples of Messiah Teachers are pastors ministering to needy congregations, group therapists working with substance abusers or parent educators presenting practical ways to prevent child abuse. Teachers serve as committee chairpersons, evangelists, and preschool teachers. They enjoy the energy of a group, and have the desire to share a unique message with those in need. Teachers fall into the Messiah Trap when the desire to communicate with others is expanded into an obligation. Teachers, especially those who deeply believe in their message, may experience great difficulty turning down opportunities to speak, teach, or perform. As with other Messiah styles, saying "no" can become an almost impossible task.

Teachers have a unique problem to face in that they must spend additional time in preparing for presentations or group activities. Only a few Teachers improvise before an audience. Consequently, a great deal of time may be needed in preparation—study, rehearsal, or writing—in addition to the time spent in the group itself. As Messiahs have difficulty limiting the number of groups or presentations, the preparation time required for each appearance adds up quickly.

Teachers can become very frustrated, especially if they pair the Teacher style with another Messiah style. Some Teachers who have a large dose of Pleaser may try to keep everyone in the group happy or be overly compliant with one or more influential members. Teacher-Givers may try to provide for the material needs of group members, thereby depleating their own limited resources. Teacher-Protectors may cater to members perceived as especially vulnerable and thus unintentionally stunt the growth of the group as a whole. Teacher-Rescuers may attempt to intervene for a particular group member or may even try to "rescue" the entire group. By taking on the group as a "client," Teacher-Counselors are easily overwhelmed by the enormity of the need. Certainly if those Messiah styles that take on the responsibility of others on a more individual basis can be overcome by the burden, Teachers—who are addicted to helping by the group load—will surely be overwhelmed.

Our society is one that nearly worships its leaders. We endow a magical quality to movie stars and superhuman power to our religious leaders, and will pay athletes astronomical sums of money to kick, dunk, or putt balls. It is easy for the Messiah Teacher to be put on a pedestal and considered special. Teachers can become entrapped in their specialness, however, if being unique allows them no place to be ordinary, to cry ordinary tears over ordinary problems. The Teacher may have no safe place to "come clean," to share genuine vulnerability and acknowledge failings. Teachers can be surrounded by people and yet agonizingly alone, trapped in the jostling crowd that wants to be touched by the Messiah. Teachers may be dismayed to find, however, that no one is touching them.

THE CRUSADER

"I'll never forget their faces," James confided, "or the smells or the sounds. Seeing those people suffering on the streets just intensifies my resolve to do everything I can to help. I wish I could take them all home with me." James's nearly-black eyes became darker still, as if his eyes had become projectors playing back the pain he had seen.

As a social worker and the director of a community-based agency, James's life revolved around his work. "Sometimes I feel so helpless when I see what's going on out there. Everyone in the program is working long hours. My wife and I seem to practically live at the agency, but still it feels like there's so much more that needs to be done. I can't rest when I feel how unjust all this is. I've got to keep going no matter what the cost." His muscular shoulders seemed to sag under the enormous weight he carried.

Like James, Crusaders are people with an acute sense of justice that propels them to action. With zeal, Crusaders lobby for stricter laws against drunk drivers, establish sanctuaries for undocumented refugees from Central America, and raise money to fight leukemia. Some Crusaders organize campaigns to legalize abortion while others organize antiabortion campaigns. While the issues selected may vary, Crusaders are invariably passionate about the social ills they have chosen to confront, intent on bringing about change.

Crusaders are susceptible to feeling frustrated over the inability to bring about change with the speed desired. This is especially painful when the Messiah is forced to watch as others suffer. When others suffer, the Crusader suffers. Crusaders are devoted, whether the commitment be to halting the nuclear arms race or lobbying for military buildup, tending to the mentally ill sleeping on our streets or providing housing for teenage prostitutes. Crusaders risk their lives smuggling Bibles into Russia and refugees into basements. In the midst of the fiery struggle, Crusaders are susceptible to feeling grief over battles lost and guilt for battles unattempted. Although beginning with a desire to empower the powerless, Crusaders often come face to face with a sense of powerlessness instead.

WHAT KIND OF MESSIAH ARE YOU?

Have you caught a glimpse of yourself in the lives of these seven Messiahs?

While the styles may differ in some ways, all seven Messiah types are helpaholics, susceptible to becoming overextended and overinvested in the lives of others. They lack the ability to set realistic limits on time, energy, or resources. Instead, Messiahs tend to feel driven to be all things to all people, responsible to meet everyone's needs with a sense of urgency.

Do you get caught up in pleasing, rescuing, giving, counseling, protecting, teaching, and crusading? If so, you may be one of the many caring people who have fallen prey to believing that you must make a lifestyle of caring for others in such a way that leaves you distraught, deprived, and alone. You may be running so fast to meet deadlines, answering phone calls, squeezing in one more client, and feeling everyone else's pain that you don't stop long enough to feel your own pain.

6. How the Messiah Trap Hurts Others

There are times when I've given all I've got and it's just not enough. The more I try, the more I seem to miss the mark. Things get muddled, people get angry with me. All I'm doing is trying to help, can't they see that?

—DALE

The Messiah Trap is full of deception. Most of the lies promoted by the Messiah Trap are hurtful to the Messiah because they undermine the Messiah's sense of self-worth, peace of mind, sense of safety, and responsibility. One of the lies of the Messiah Trap, however, is damaging to others, to those very people the Messiah tries to help. The Messiah Trap asserts that when the Messiah "helps" others, they are benefited. The truth of the matter is, *Messiahs hurt when they help.*

Messiahs pretend that they are loving others when they are actually suffering from a powerfully destructive addiction. Being addicted to helping other people may not seem like such a terrible malady. After all, how can helping be a harmful thing? Do not be deceived by the *content* of this addiction. It is an addiction, nevertheless, and this fact must not be minimized.

When you are controlled by the Messiah Trap, you are out of control of your choices, your feelings, and the effect you have on others. Love is not the motivation of someone caught in the Messiah Trap. Messiahs may preach eloquent sermons to their parishioners, teach complicated truths to their students, unravel psychological mysteries for their clients, give their last dime to the poor, and more—but not out of love. On the contrary, feelings of inadequacy and powerlessness, obligation and rage motivate the Messiah. Being a "helpaholic" can be just as addictive, compulsive, and destructive as any other addiction.

To put it bluntly, the Messiah uses other people to work out his or her own inner pain. The compulsion to bond with people who remind Messiahs of themselves is motivated by the need to feel other people's pain in order for Messiahs to feel their own. Messiahs catch a glimpse of their wounds in the tears of others, hear an echo of their grief in the sobs of a friend. This ugly truth is hidden by the promotion of the Messiah's "good deeds."

The apostle Paul summed up the Messiah dilemma succinctly when he wrote about love in 1 Corinthians 13:

"If I speak with the tongues of men and of angels, but have not love, I am only a resounding gong or a clanging cymbal. If I have the gift of prophecy and can fathom all mysteries and all knowledge, and if I have a faith that can move mountains, but have not love, I am nothing. If I give all I possess to the poor and surrender my body to the flames, but have not love, I gain nothing.

He describes the value placed on external "do-gooder" activities that are not motivated by love—they are worthless. Messiahs do *good things* for the *wrong reasons*, and therefore the best of their efforts prove futile.

Since the impetus for Messiah activities is not love, the impact of such efforts is also devoid of love. When entrapped, the Messiah finds it difficult to see that such help given to others is equally entrapping. Since they unconsciously focus on self-need, Messiahs tend to misinterpret the needs of others. *Messiahs tend to give to others what they so desperately need to receive themselves.* What others may actually need often goes unnoticed as the Messiah misjudges the situation. It is impossible to genuinely give to receive love when caught in the Messiah Trap.

THE PLEASER—BLOCKING HONEST COMMUNICATION

The deep frown lines in Elizabeth's face underscored her disappointment and fatigue. The polish on several of her nails was chipped as her hands, which usually gripped her day planner as if ready for action, lay limply in her lap. Through reddened, tired eyes, Elizabeth described her attempt at making friends: "I wanted everything about the weekend to be perfect. Each detail was planned from start to finish. I had thought through who to invite so that there would be a complementary mix of personalities as well as an equal number of men and women, with couples and singles."

Elizabeth had reached out to others the only way she knew how—by putting herself in a helper role. She had tried to organize the perfect weekend getaway. Now she was experiencing the pain that results from trying to earn acceptance by attempting to please others.

"I set up special outings that were prepaid with discounts for group rates. The condo we rented had a VCR with plenty of videos. Even the meal preparation schedule was designed so that we only had to do kitchen duty once the entire weekend. Everyone received a colorful flier describing every aspect of the trip. I thought I'd finally feel a part of the group after this weekend."

"At the last minute, one couple and two of the single men called me to say they could not attend. Each had valid reasons but this threw all my plans out of sync. Instead of the balanced group I had so painstakingly arranged, we now had a cabin filled with four women and two men. We lost our discount on two of the special outings because the group was too small to qualify. Worst of all," she complained glancing down at her damaged manicure, "we each had to do kitchen duty several times during the trip. I felt awful."

Leaning forward, Elizabeth began to release some of the feelings she had carefully held captive all weekend. "What really bothered me about the situation was the way the group responded to me. Whenever I was in the room, everyone acted happy and tried to tell me they were having a fine time in spite of it all. I knew they were miserable. No one would admit to me how they really felt. Once, when they thought I was up in the loft, I heard Sylvia say, 'What a washout of a weekend. I wish I could just head on home.' Adam said, 'Yeah, me too. But that would really hurt Elizabeth's feelings. We can go on pretending. The weekend's almost over.'

"I felt absolutely humiliated," Elizabeth confessed.

Elizabeth was learning that relationships promoted by Pleasers are, by their very nature, dishonest. Pleasers pretend to be powerful enough to make other people happy and, interestingly enough, other people tend to join in the charade. Elizabeth believed she could make people like her by planning the perfect weekend. Her fantasy crashed in on her when she found she couldn't control all the variables. When her efforts did not result in pleasing her friends with the perfect weekend, Elizabeth felt she had failed. Worse still, she felt unloved.

When caught up in the Messiah Trap, Messiahs are unable to give or receive love. Busy in the task of pretending to please and be pleased, the focus is not on expressing feelings to one another. Pleasers do not reveal themselves or risk being known. Instead, Pleasers say what they think will please others in much the same way that Elizabeth's friends tried to act *as if* Elizabeth had pleased them. There is little concern for the truth when one needs to generate positive response from others.

This addiction can be so compelling that Pleasers may go to any length to please. They may manipulate, paint on false faces, swallow feelings, even lie. Pleasers unknowingly sacrifice chances for genuine communion for a shabby replica. Elizabeth tried to make friends through her Messiah behavior but succeeded only in damaging those budding relationships. No one is assisted when a Pleaser swings into action. The opportunity for intimacy is traded for the illusion that the Pleaser has made someone else happy.

THE RESCUER—ENCOURAGING FEELINGS OF HELPLESSNESS IN OTHERS

"It has been one thing after another today!" Dale complained. "First I somehow scheduled two hearings for the same morning. Ever try to be in two courtrooms at the same time? And then Sally called again, remember her? The client I told you about who is fighting for custody of her kids? Well, she called, crying, and said she needed to see me right away, so I squeezed her in at lunch. Of course, that threw the rest of my appointment schedule off, and I've been working on several cases . . . and" Dale paused and took a deep breath. "Phew! One crises after another." Looking at his watch, he frowned, "And I've already missed half of my session."

"Do you feel comfortable with trading half of your time away in order to take care of other people?" I asked.

Turning his hands up in helplessness, he shrugged, "What else could I do? These people really needed me, especially Sally."

When I asked how it happened that his needs were sacrificed in order to meet someone else's, Dale became irritated. "What am I supposed to say to Sally when she's sobbing about how her husband threatened to beat her? I'll schedule you in next Tuesday? This was a crisis. She relies on me now to help get her through this divorce. There are more papers to file, plus a restraining order since his threat last night."

Dale presented Sally as a woman who was dependent on him for her survival. His first impression of Sally was more positive. "She seemed like many of the divorce cases I take on—she was upset and in shock but appeared to be handling things fairly well. The longer she has been separated from her husband, however, the more she has been relying on me. She depended on her husband for so many things. She doesn't even know how to balance her checkbook. So, once a month now she brings all her paperwork in to the office, and I balance her books."

He smiled. "She said she didn't know what she would do without me. She feels so helpless." Growing stern once more he challenged, "How can you suggest that I abandon this woman?"

Dale was caught up in the delusion of the Messiah Trap, which was damaging both himself and Sally, the woman he was trying to help. This delusion has several components.

First, Dale was trying to earn his worth by rescuing other people from real and imagined crises. So Dale was in continuous need of people in crisis. Rescuers tend to associate themselves with situations or organizations that specialize in crises. As professionals, Rescuers may be doctors in hospital emergency rooms, highway patrol officers who respond to traffic accidents or social workers at abortion counseling clinics. As paraprofessionals, Rescuers may volunteer for the teen suicide hotline or provide support services to families of children with terminal illnesses. As laypeople, Rescuers may associate with clubs and groups that focus on crisis situations such as substance abuse recovery support groups or churches with programs for the homeless and mentally ill. By opening a law practice specializing in divorce cases, Dale assured himself an endless supply of clients in crisis. Rescuers are attracted to situations that attract people in crisis.

Secondly, his addiction to rescuing propelled Dale to go beyond proper boundaries, creating a special expectation on the part of those he rescued. Dale, as Messiah, bonded with clients, like Sally, who were in search of a Messiah. It is uncanny how Messiahs and people who want a Messiah to rescue them can find one another.

Messiahs often develop long-term relationships with these people, feeling both trapped and gratified by their need for care. Rescuers may be expected to rescue a parent from a drinking problem or an adult child from financial stress. They may have friends call only when they are in crisis, maybe one who has called at least five times this month.

Thirdly, Dale felt that he had to choose between having his needs met and caring for the needs of others. Out of his craving for affirmation, Dale overscheduled his day, attracted crisis situations, and cultivated dependent relationships. When he was confronted with attending to his own needs *directly* (such as coming to his counseling session on time) or by gaining a sense of worth *indirectly* (by playing the Rescuer with Sally), he continually chose the way of the Messiah Trap. Many Messiahs, like Dale, do not recognize that personal needs do not conflict with the needs of others. This conflict exists only within the Messiah Trap. To explain what I mean, let me move to the fourth delusion to which Dale had fallen prey.

Dale believed that when he rescued Sally he was helping her. He was not. When he provided professional services, he was treating Sally with dignity and genuine assistance. By balancing her checkbook, however, he was treating her like an incompetent victim. His actions underscored her low self-esteem and intensified her fear that she couldn't cope without a man in her life. When he came running to her every call, he showed her that he believed she was incapable of protecting herself and managing her own life as an adult. He was crippling Sally's growth each time he rescued her.

While Dale was in the Messiah Trap, he saw only two choices—he had to either rescue or abandon Sally. He was blind to the many ways he could have genuinely loved and helped her. Dale could have responded to this needy woman in a non-Messiah manner, which may have included referring her to a community college program designed to assist women in transition, helping her find a support group for divorcing parents, or encouraging her to have a friend instruct her in how to care for her finances. There were a variety of ways Dale could have helped facilitate Sally's growth and encouraged her to take responsibility for her own life. Instead, Dale fell into the trap of hurting the very person he was trying to help.

THE CRUSADER—IS ANGRY AT OTHERS WHO AREN'T DEDICATED TO THE CAUSE

"I'm upset by a problem at work," James began. "I just had the most distressing conversation with one of our advocacy workers. Jill is her name. When I first met her, her life was pretty much of a mess. She came from a rough background and was always in trouble. But I could see her potential and hung in there with her. Jill really responded to the care we gave her. We even gave her a job at the agency. What a transformation! Always there when we need her. She hangs in like a trooper and has become one of our best front-line workers. At least I thought she had, until recently."

He continued with pain in his eyes. "We have been frantically working on a funding proposal that was due this afternoon at five. The whole staff was at the agency all weekend, practically around the clock pulling this thing together. The only person who didn't show up was Jill. This morning the group was exhausted but we still needed to make copies and collate the pages. In walks Jill, no apology, no explanation about where she was all weekend, nothing! She came up to me with a big smile and asked what she could do to help out, and I was furious!"

"I asked her why she hadn't been here all weekend, and she just gave me this disgusted look and said that she had already worked forty hours last week and wasn't scheduled to work weekends. Can you believe that?" James glared up at me. "I told her that her job was done when the job was finished, not when she had put in a few hours. She shook her head and walked away. I just don't understand her attitude."

Crusaders like James are people of deep commitment who become consumed by the crusade. At times the cost is great and the risks are grave. When the stakes are high, Crusaders often become single-minded in their devotion. Often the passion for the cause so permeates the Crusader that there is no longer room for any other passion. The selected crusade becomes the focal point of the Crusader's life.

When this occurs, Crusaders are especially susceptible to falling captive to anger. It is easy for those who believe intensely to become enraged at unnecessary suffering—children with starving, crying eyes, young lives destroyed by drugs, or people dying alone in unheated apartments. Crusaders feel a righteous anger, one that motivates them to action. Anger is a powerful, often consuming emotion, however, and the Crusader may find that rage is the only emotion he or she is able to feel. I call it "Crusader's Rage."

Crusader's Rage, like a contagious disease, can spread from hatred for injustice to hatred of people. Most often, other groups are fighting in opposition to or standing in the way of the cause. It is far too easy to lose sight of the issue and begin to hate those who oppose the crusade. While beginning as *lovers of justice,* Crusaders can become *haters of people* and yet never notice that they have slipped into this ugliness. Crusaders may deceive themselves into believing they are still fighting in a positive way because they are committed to a positive end when they have actually become addicted to the crusade.

Eventually Crusader's Rage may be directed at co-workers. James had fallen into this trap. "I tried to talk with Jill later," he continued, "but we didn't get very far. She had the nerve to say that she was willing to work the hours she was paid to work. If I wanted her to work more hours, she would expect to be paid overtime! She knows we are working on a shoestring. I couldn't believe she was so materialistic and would expect to be paid more even though it would mean less food for the hungry! It broke my heart."

Like James, Crusaders are often blinded by their addiction and unknowingly promote the lies of the Messiah Trap with fervor. Crusaders believe that only they and their committed group can bring about the change needed (Side 1) and that nothing is more important than the cause—even the needs of those with whom the Crusader works (Side 2). If a co-worker does not act in accordance with the lies of the Messiah Trap— does not act as if the entire world depends on him or her and also insists on having their own needs met—Crusaders often feel betrayed and angry. It is easy for Crusaders to lose sight of the fact that those with whom they work are *people*—with legitimate needs and intrinsic worth. For Crusaders, however, co-workers become means to an end, workhorses, objects.

For the Crusader, nothing but total commitment and devotion to the cause is tolerated. Crusaders adopt an "If you're not with us, you must be against us" position. Everyone must declare their loyalties—all or nothing, black and white, good or bad. Co-workers are expected to sacrifice everything, and I do mean *everything*, for the cause— friends, family, health, money. In leadership positions, Crusaders tend to overwork and underpay their staff. There is no higher burnout rate than in those organizations run by Crusaders.

And when co-workers can no longer stand the strain and unrealistic demands placed on them, do Crusaders see the error of their ways? No. Usually the Crusaders feel betrayed.

Over the years, I have worked in a wide variety of social service and church- related groups committed to various worthy causes. While these agencies have certainly contributed to the lives of their clientele, it has been my observation that Crusader's Rage has damaged a number of the staff. Marriages of co-workers have crumbled because no time was allowed for the marriage to be nurtured, the health of co-workers has broken because no time was allowed for rest, and the emotional and spiritual lives of co-workers have eroded because no time was allowed for solitude. All too often Crusaders win the crusade but neglect to count the many co-workers who were crusade casualties, sacrificed along the way.

THE GIVER—ATTEMPTING TO CONTROL OTHERS VIA GIFTGIVING

"I feel like an empty pit," Alicia cried. "My younger sister Tanya's in trouble again, and I want to help her. It's just that I feel like I've given everything I have away."

Rubbing her hands over the elbows of her thread-bare sweater, she sighed. "Tanya has asked me to co-sign for a car. Her credit is so bad that, even with her job and all no one would loan her the money. I said that I would but she would have to show me her bank statement each month as proof that she had made her car payments. I want to know where all this money is going. She started yelling at me, saying I had no right to try to tell her what to do. I told her I had every right as long as she was living off my money. She finally came to her senses and agreed."

"I don't know what's the matter with her." Alicia complained. "Tanya is always getting into financial trouble. I don't know what she does with her money. She has a good job, but that doesn't seem to matter. She's always coming up short at the end of the month." Alicia tilted her head and frowned, "That's the only time I see her these days—at the end of the month when she's out of money or when she needs a free meal."

On the surface, Givers like Alicia may appear to be helping. But a person who receives what a Messiah Giver has to give actually loses—by relinquishing control over his or her own life. The Giver takes control. When the Messiah takes over for others, the message conveyed is: Those receiving assistance are incapable of caring for themselves. The Messiah communicates to others that they are inferior and therefore they need the Messiah to take care of them. Help is offered at a price. While Givers may appear to be giving, they are actually taking—taking responsibility for others, taking control over them, and taking away their self-esteem.

Alicia was teaching her younger sister a damaging lesson. Tanya learned that her actions did not have serious consequences because someone else stronger would cover for her mistakes and irresponsibility. Alicia contributed to Tanya's growing up dependent and manipulative.

By providing Tanya with cash and meals Alicia "bought" regular visits from her sister. Alicia realized that Tanya would not visit her if there were not a trade. Their relationship was not one of balanced, loving intimacy. It was based on Alicia's willingness to take responsibility for Tanya, and they mislabeled this charade as *love*.

THE PROTECTOR—WITHHOLDING INFORMATION OR BREAKING CONFIDENTIALITY

"Paul, would you tell me more about what your childhood was like? I asked as our session began.

Looking at his wife, Cindi, he recalled, "I thought I had a happy family until I was around eight, when my dad abruptly moved out. I had never heard them fight, not once. My mother said they had wanted to protect me from their problems."

A cynical smile crept across Paul's face. "That's a joke! One day I came home from school and my dad was packing up his car. I asked him where he was going. He got tears in his eyes and said that he was going on a trip. He didn't even tell me the truth when I asked him. He was leaving for good but led me to believe he was going away for a few days. You could never know how much it hurt for me to realize that not only was he not coming back, but he had lied to me as well."

Cindi accused, "Paul, how can you hurt me the same way?"

Paul stared at her, bewildered. Cindi continued, "Knowing that people hurt you when you were a child by withholding the truth doesn't seem to stop you from doing the very same thing to me."

"When have I hurt you?" he asked.

"What about last week?" she accused. "You knew that my mother had gone into the hospital again. You didn't tell me."

Paul tried to defend himself. "I didn't want you to worry."

"Why not?" Cindi continued. "Do you think I am so fragile that I can't face the truth? By your not telling me, I missed being at the hospital with her. You *hurt* me when you 'protect' me."

The most common way that people attempt to protect others is by keeping potentially hurtful information secret. Protectors guard the family secrets. Protectors don't admit that Mom has a drinking problem, that Uncle Jerry has lost another job, or that Sister's husband is having an affair. Instead of the truth, Protectors tell each other that Aunt Tillie needs her Valium for her back pain and that the bruises on the grandchildren's legs are due to another accident. Protectors are those who go through life guarding the secret that Granddad molested them when they were children, because it would break Grandma's heart if she ever found out the truth.

Paul learned from his parents to be a Protector. Even though he suffered from the damaging effects of the "protection" of his parents, he had difficulty seeing how his efforts to "protect" his wife were equally hurtful. Like Paul, Protectors are notorious for hiding the truth from others—and from hiding the truth from themselves. Intimacy is based on honesty and open communication. As long as the Protector is caught in the Messiah Trap, however, he or she is caught in a web of distortions and therefore intimacy is not possible.

Another trap Protectors fall into is passing on *too much* information. Very often, Protectors are caught between loyalties. Paul described to me a situation in which one of his co-workers, Linda, told Paul about her dissatisfaction with Alice's poor work performance (an office staff member). Linda was struggling with the question of whether or not she should fire Alice. Paul wanted to protect Alice from being fired, so he told her what Linda had said. Paul assumed Alice would keep the source of the information confidential. (It is interesting to note that Paul broke Linda's confidentiality but expected Alice to protect his.) Alice, however, went straight to Linda, confronted her about her job security, and in the process let it slip that Paul was the one who spilled the goods. In an effort to protect Alice, Paul violated Linda's trust, and in an effort to protect herself Alice violated Paul's.

Protectors, like Paul, unintentionally damage relationships by erroneously judging what is and what is not hurtful to someone else. Protectors tend to withhold the truth when it is time to speak honestly, and to pass on information that is not appropriate to share—all under the name of caring.

THE COUNSELOR—PROMOTES ONE-SIDED INTIMACY

Reluctantly and rather defiantly, Diedre's sister stepped through my office door. Refusing to sit down—"Because I'm not staying long"—Andrea said, "I suppose you're going to tell me what to do, too, huh?" While Diedre was busy counseling nearly everyone in her life, she was having difficulty "getting through" to her sister. She asked Andrea to talk with me, hoping we could bridge the chasm growing between them.

Andrea blamed the distance she felt from her sister on Diedre's tendency to "counsel" her rather than spend time with her. Andrea complained, "I feel like I have to be in trouble for her even to notice me. I don't see her often, but when I do she always starts the conversation with a question like 'So what seems to be the problem here?' Sometimes I don't have problems. Sometimes I just want to be with my sister and talk about nothing. But for my sister to stay interested in me, I have to come up with something for her to help me with, or she just leaves me behind as she goes off to help someone else."

Diedre is not alone in this tendency. I have observed ministers who try to act as pastor to their spouses, teachers who try to instruct their friends, and administrators who manage family outings like a board meeting. Addicted to helping, Counselors often try to turn every encounter into a counseling session. As a consequence, these relationships are hindered, and those who genuinely need intimacy from the Counselor are often left wanting.

Messiah Counselors become masters of one-sided intimacy. While Counselors set up relationships that involve deep caring and emotional connection, they are often careful that the vulnerability is experienced by others, not by themselves. Others are expected to disclose their own feelings while the Counselors hide safely behind the Messiah role.

Because the emotional connection between Counselor and those counseled can be intense and even exhilarating, it is easy for Counselors to emerge with the sense that they have deeply touched another human being. As a Counselor, you may have touched them, but you have kept them from touching you. While counselees give access to their deepest selves, the Counselor does not return the favor. Clients may display courage but a Counselor hides his or her issues from view. Wounds are exposed, cleaned out, and allowed to heal. But the wounds are not the Counselor's—whose wounds are still buried deep, festering and sore.

Since Messiahs have chosen the indirect route for growth—*indirect and ineffective*—Counselors are often driven to bond with people who remind them of themselves. When a Messiah Counselor comforts a frightened child, it is in the attempt to console the Counselor's own trembling inner child. When assisting a rape victim to regain a sense of safety, the Counselor is trying to empower the victim within him or herself. The resolution of other people's marital tension can offer hope to the Counselor's own troubled relationships. By exerting power in someone else's life, the Counselor pretends to have gained more personal control.

Since Counselors are deeply dependent on those counseled, Counselors need others to have problems (problems that are small enough for the Counselor to solve) and want others to grow (but not too much). It would not be desirable for counselees to grow past the Counselor and thereby leave the Counselor alone to confront his or her own pain directly. Consequently, Counselors tend to foster dependency and hinder the growth of others.

This dependency on the problems of other people can damage

the Counselor's own relationships. Because Diedre so desperately needed problems to solve, she was unintentionally hurting her sister. Andrea had a legitimate need for intimacy with her sister, but Diedre could not meet her on a mutual basis. Diedre only knew how to set up relationships with one-sided intimacy. For Andrea to relate on Diedre's terms, Andrea would have to sacrifice her own growth. Andrea would have had to become dependent on her sister and to provide Diedre with problems to solve. When Andrea had no "problems," Andrea had no place in Diedre's life.

While Messiah Counselors claim to be helping others, they are really involved in maintaining a fragile sense of well-being. Inner growth, as a personal experience with its required courage and risk, is quite foreign to the Messiah. While observing others on the front lines, battling with tears in their eyes against their inner fears, Messiah Counselors have not left home and hearth to personally travel deep into those dark inner regions. Because they have only an armchair experience of growth, Counselors can take counselees and personal relationships only so far. Many counselees are stunted and entrapped by the Counselor's own inability to progress. The people in the Counselor's life must break free if they choose to grow. Such losses can be confusing and extremely painful to Counselors who can't understand why they are being left behind. Some, like Andrea, do move on but feel the loss of needed intimacy and a wound where there could have been love.

THE TEACHER—AVOIDS INTIMACY BY BEING "ON STAGE"

Gary was stretched out on the couch, holding a pillow over his chest as he stared at the ceiling. Life seemed to be crashing in on him, and he couldn't understand why, since he had done everything "right." He had been the best son he thought he could be to his mother. The week after he graduated from college, Gary had married Annie, his childhood sweetheart. He went on to complete a doctoral degree and quickly landed a position with a prestigious university. During his twenty years in teaching, Gary had proven himself a talented professor, public speaker, and writer. He was known for the special interest he showed in his students.

Annie and Gary were the proud parents of two sons. As far as he had been concerned, his professional and personal life had been progressing smoothly.

Gary's rosy outlook ended abruptly and painfully one afternoon. The afternoon began innocently enough. "I was racing to the airport because I thought Pat, one of the students I had been working with, was dropping out of school and intending to leave town. I get invested in many of my students. Even so, Pat was special to me. I put a great deal of time and energy into him." Gary told me he had been thinking through what he would say at the airport, when he glanced casually at the hotels and restaurants that lined the main street to the airport. His eye caught the image of a familiar car parked in a motel lot. The car belonged to his wife, Annie.

"I never made it to the airport. I spent the rest of the day and most of the night driving by myself trying to erase the scene I had just witnessed. My only desire was to forget seeing another man holding Annie in his arms." Even though six months had passed since the confrontation at the hotel, his pain was fresh and severe.

Crossing his arms over the pillow, he sighed. "Annie told me she couldn't handle the loneliness anymore, that's why she turned to that guy. With him, she feels important. She said I make her feel like she's just a part of my audience. To quote her, she said, 'I'm tired of standing on the side lines clapping, hoping you'll notice I'm there.' "

Gary complained, "I don't understand what she wants from me. She just doesn't appreciate all I do for her. I feel like I'm a good husband. I've never gone out on her and I'm a good provider. What about all the extra speaking engagements I took on so we could afford the new house? She keeps saying she needs more, but I just don't know what that is."

"It's not like I ignore her. I take her to many of the retreats and conferences where I'm speaking. I don't understand why she's so disgruntled, none of her friends travel as much as she does. None of their husbands travel with their work like I do."

Messiahs mistakenly believe that intimacy with another person is based on taking care of them or including them in their addicted, caregiving activities. When his wife asked him for intimacy, Gary hadn't the slightest clue as to what Annie meant. He thought that when he allowed his wife to watch him while he performed his Messiah role, he was relating to her on an intimate level. He pointed to the number of times Annie was allowed to listen to him speak before large audiences, the various cities she followed behind him as a fan, as evidence of the depth of their communication.

As with other types of Messiahs, Teachers are trying to earn a sense of worth and control through a caregiving role. Messiah Teachers feel most comfortable when in front of a group of people, either in some type of leadership or performing role. As the energy flows between the Teacher and the audience, the Teacher is in tune with the pulse of the crowd. After making a presentation, preaching a sermon, or performing a concert, a feeling of rejuvenation often results. It is easy to become deeply invested in the group process of the therapy group, Sunday School class, or task force meetings.

One reason Teachers are so connected to group energy and response is the level of their dependency on group approval. What could be more exhilarating than the cheers of the crowd? Certainly the admiration of a group of people can help the Messiah believe he or she is someone special—at least until the applause dies down. In order to maintain a sense of well-being, Teachers can find themselves continually hungry for a steady diet of public appearances.

While other Messiah styles tend to receive rewards on a one-to-one basis, Teachers perform their role before audiences and so the feedback received is on a grander scale. This intense interaction between the Teacher and the group is often mistaken for intimacy. The excitement of the crowd may lull the Teacher into a false feeling of closeness. While the Teacher may affect the lives of many, no one has the opportunity for genuine intimacy with a Messiah Teacher.

Gary had grown numb to the need for intimacy in his life as he filled every waking hour in pursuit of performing before a crowd. He not only enjoyed the spotlight, but he needed the spotlight in order to feel special. Gary had little time for his wife and family. Gary's story is not unusual. We can see this pattern in the lives of many public personalities—politicians, missionaries, entertainers—who put their public lives first. Once we understand that the

Teacher is motivated by a deep need for approval, it becomes clear why he or she neglects the family. How could the request for vulnerability from a spouse compete with the cheers of the crowd? How could the opportunity to play a game with a ten year old or listen to the chatter of a teenager compete with the adoration of an audience? Teachers may tell themselves there is a job to do, a gospel to preach, a lecture to give, or a buck to earn, but underneath this self-deception is an addiction based on the need to earn a sense of worth and a fear of genuine intimacy.

HOW THE MESSIAH TRAP HURTS OTHERS

Blinded by their addiction, Messiahs want to believe that they are helping others. Unfortunately, others are hurt, not helped, by the helpaholic. The first side of the Messiah Trap generates feelings of helplessness. As a consequence, Messiahs are motivated to control the lives of others. Those the Messiah tries to heal are crippled, those "assisted" are actually hindered.

The second side of the Messiah Trap undermines self-esteem. In an attempt to combat these feelings of worthlessness, the Messiah undermines the self-esteem of others. The Messiah cannot give what the Messiah does not have—and the Messiah does not have high self-regard.

If you are caught in the Messiah Trap, it is critical, for the welfare of others, that you face the damage you are unintentionally promoting. Are you promoting dishonest relationships under the guise of pleasing others? Perhaps you are fostering feelings of dependency or encouraging irresponsibility in others. Do you find yourself enraged at those with whom you work, for their lack of devotion? Could it be that your anger is based on the lies of the Messiah Trap, and that you resent the fact that others are free of its lies? In an attempt to protect others, are you hiding the truth? Or maybe breaking a confidence? Do you hide from intimacy by getting others to open up or by performing before a crowd?

Granted, these issues are difficult to face. But until you break free of the Messiah Trap with its addiction and its deceptions, you will hurt those you want to help and abandon those you long to embrace.

7. How to Escape the Messiah Trap

I can seen how I'm hurting myself and everyone else by playing the
Messiah. I want to break out of this but I just don't know how. I feel so . . .
trapped.

—PAUL

Throughout this book I have referred to the Messiah Trap as
something that has had a hold on the Messiah. It is now time to acknowledge that the Messiah is the one holding onto the Messiah
Trap. The Messiah has a tight grip on this distorted view of reality
with its empty promise of power and a sense of worth. It can be
frightening to let go of the lies of Messiah Trap and reach out for
something new. As your fingers loosen their hold on the lies you may
have believed all your life, there is no guarantee that you will now
get a hold on the truth. Letting go of the Messiah Trap is a risk,
there is no denying that. It is a risk, however, that I urge you to take.

ACKNOWLEDGE THAT YOU ARE CAUGHT IN THE MESSIAH TRAP

The first step in letting go of the Messiah Trap is admitting you
are caught in its powerful hold. I remember how difficult it was for
me to first admit that I was a helpaholic. It was hard for me then,
and it is even difficult at times for me now. When I tell people about
my addiction often their eyes will grow cold and I sense they don't
want to hear anymore. I suspect that their reaction, in part, has to
do with the kind of addiction with which we Messiahs struggle.

Being addicted to helping is so common, yet it is one of those
problems seldom discussed. If I were addicted to drugs or alcohol,
I'd have groups like Alcoholics Anonymous and substance abuse
treatment programs to help me. If I were addicted to food or
gambling or even sex, there would be people sharing my problem,
to accept and help me break free. But there are no Messiah Anon-

ymous groups waiting for us Messiahs. Why not? We are too busy pretending we have no problems, too busy focusing on everyone else's addictions, to face our own and to offer genuine help to each other.

ASK FOR HELP

The next step in letting go of the Messiah Trap is going for help. Messiahs inevitably try to deal with their own issues by themselves. But be warned, *I have never seen a Messiah let go of the Trap without assistance.* You cannot successfully cope with this addiction all by yourself.

WHY IS ASKING FOR HELP SO DIFFICULT?

Asking for help is one of the most difficult tasks a Messiah can face. Messiahs have been hurt. They have trusted and have been deceived. Now, armored in Messiah suits, they have made every effort to keep these painful experiences from happening again.

One of the ways Messiahs try to avoid being rehurt is by pretending that they were never hurt in the first place. Messiahs pretend to be strong, a cut above the others, somehow insulated from life's assaults. When I believe the lies of the Messiah Trap, I feel that I am the strongest—in fact, I am the *only* person who can deal effectively with a particular difficult situation. If I don't take care of the people in my life, who else will? When in the Messiah Trap, I am convinced that I can count on no one else but myself.

Since the Messiah Trap deceives me into thinking that only I am competent and trustworthy, I am left with no one to turn to when I need help. Why should I entrust my weakness and fears to the hands of those I consider to be less able to cope with life than myself? Being a Messiah in trouble can be lonely and frightening, even terrifying. Messiahs fear that there are no arms strong enough to hold on while they cry, no one wise enough to guide them through the murkiness, no heart patient enough to see them through the long and turbulent journey.

OVERSENSITIVITY TO GUILT

Messiahs feel guilty for just about everything.

Although Messiahs may deal compassionately with the failings of others, they demand nothing less than perfection from themselves. I have often heard Messiahs state that they judge themselves on a "higher" standard due to their "position" (teacher, pastor, therapist, etc.). As a result of this unrealistic standard for success (by pretending to be gods), Messiahs have great difficulty discerning the actual degree of severity of their transgressions. Messiahs can become extremely harsh with themselves when they fall short of perfection. Acting as prosecutor, judge, and jury, Messiahs rarely provide themselves with a defense, so it is no surprise that Messiahs find themselves "guilty"!

If a Messiah should overcome the first obstacle to getting help by finally trusting another person to care, this second force of guilt threatens to push him or her back into silent suffering. Why expose one's failings and ugliness to anyone else? As Messiahs, we feel certain that others would recoil in horror if they knew the evil fantasies that flitted through our minds, the forbidden impulses we try desperately to control, and the distressing feelings we attempt to suppress. If Messiahs agonize over trivial transgressions such as being fifteen minutes late to an appointment or failing to return a phone call, how open can they expect to be with revealing the truly dark sides of their lives?

OVERSENSITIVITY TO SHAME

Shame, in contrast to guilt, is the feeling that we, not merely our conduct, are unacceptable. It is a deep and primitive feeling that can be triggered by simple things. We may be in a room of people who laugh at a joke we don't understand or we may find the zipper in our pants is undone. Shame is what we feel when we mispronounce a word, drip soup on our chins, or sneeze without the protection of a tissue. Any of these common experiences can cause us to wish we could crawl into a hole and hide. Shame comes on us with waves of humiliation and feelings of inadequacy. We are just not good enough.

There is nothing more humiliating for a Messiah than to admit that he or she is, for whatever reason, unable to take care of someone else. What could be more upsetting for Pleasers than to find out that someone was made unhappy by their actions. What could be more embarrassing for Givers than to be financially unable to provide a request for assistance? If someone is hurt, Messiahs will agonize if unable to protect or rescue them. Counselors will stutter and falter should a client present a problem too complicated to unravel. A Teacher may vow never to go before another group when confronted with a bright student who asks questions the Messiah cannot answer. And Crusaders hide in disgrace when yet another battle is lost.

The feelings Messiahs feel in these situations go beyond guilt. The inner jury not only declares the Messiah's actions as bad but also declares the Messiah a failure as a human being. Feelings of shame push him or her deeper into the Messiah Trap as the fear, exposure, humiliation, and rejection becomes overwhelming.

WHY IS ASKING FOR HELP SO IMPORTANT?

Since these agonizing and overwhelming feelings of fear, guilt, and shame can be triggered so easily, it is understandable that a Messiah resists becoming vulnerable to another person. It may be quite tempting at this point to put this book down, wander off, and tell yourself that you are capable of dealing with your problems by yourself. After all, you have been juggling the lives of everyone else you know—how hard could it be to resolve a little thing like the Messiah Trap? Why is it important, even necessary, that you reach out for help?

TAKING YOUR TURN

Let's return to the two-sided lie of the Messiah Trap in order to answer that question. As you recall, the Messiah Trap asserts two contradictory beliefs—Side 1: "If I didn't do it, it won't get done," and Side 2: "Everyone else's needs take priority over mine." When you are in the Messiah Trap, you feel set apart from other people. On one hand, you are superior and more powerful, while on the other you are unimportant and, at best, last in line. Messiahs alternate between feeling better and worse than everyone else, looking up to some and down on others. Messiahs never look anyone straight in the eye, as an equal.

An integral part of letting go of the Messiah Trap is embracing a common bond with others. You need to be able to say, to at least one other human being, "I am just like you, no better and no worse." The Messiah must relinquish hold on an inflated sense of power as well as an exaggerated view of frailty. No longer do you have to wait until everyone else is satisfied. You have waited long enough. It is now your turn.

YOU NEED HELP

A second reason why it is important to reach out for help is simply because you *need* it. If you are caught in the Messiah Trap, you are struggling with an addiction. By letting go of the Messiah Trap, you also let go of your way of viewing the world and yourself in it. This is no simple task. You may find yourself scrutinizing much of what was once trusted to be true—your identity, the way you conduct your relationships, your choice of profession, and your spiritual beliefs. You may re-examine your childhood, which may confront you with memories and feelings you have spent your entire life trying to avoid. Feelings may be triggered that are too frightening and confusing to face alone.

YOU DESERVE HELP

Not only do you *need* help, you *deserve* help. By asking someone for assistance, you are declaring your worth. Messiahs are important enough to warrant time, attention, and tender, loving care. Your story is worth listening to simply because it is yours. Each of us has a story of courage, of dignity, of sadness and triumph. When we tell our stories, we treat ourselves as the valuable creatures we are and emerge with a deeper sense of our common humanity and of our worth.

WHO CAN YOU ASK FOR HELP?

I have found that the most beneficial situation for letting go of the Messiah Trap is a combination of individual counseling and a peer support group (a type of "Messiahs Anonymous" group). Both are important and helpful, for different reasons.

Individual counseling is especially valuable at the beginning stages of letting go of the Messiah Trap. Messiahs need to explore private, locked-away places that may not be on the map you received from your family, your friends, or your professional training. You will need to start at the beginning, and you may uncover things you never thought existed. It is especially helpful to have a trained psychotherapist or spiritual director who can help you chart this uncharted course.

In addition to individual counseling, I have found support groups invaluable. In individual counseling, you receive individual care as you discard the lies of the Messiah Trap. In a support group, you *experience* a common bond with other people. You will be able to experience, at first hand, what it feels like to be a peer, someone of equal value and equal power. Being with other Messiahs can be one of the most liberating experiences a Messiah can have. It can also be one of the most anxiety producing, if you are unaccustomed to being with others who feel and act as you do. It is common to feel rather "ordinary" when you listen to others describe how burdened they feel with the cares of the world.

Participating in a support group helps the Messiah work through misconceptions about power and worth—you do not have to be different to be worthwhile. (Specific steps you may take in selecting a therapist and how to set up a support group are described in Appendix A, "How to Find the Help You Need.")

TAKE THE RISK OF HEALING

Make no mistake about it, the journey you must embark on in order to let go of the lies of the Messiah Trap is not easy. It may be filled with feelings you never knew you could feel, more pain than you believed you could bear, more confusion than you hoped to sort through, and more isolation than could be endured. When you let go of the Messiah Trap, however, you will be free for the first time to embrace your freedom, your worth, and the joys of intimacy. The journey of healing involves, at least, the following seven tasks:

1. Acknowledge your need for spiritual assistance
2. Cooperate with the process of growth
3. Attend to your inner work
4. Listen to the hurting child inside
5. Identify your own needs and wants
6. Acknowledge the damage done to others
7. Learn to accept love and nurturance

1. ACKNOWLEDGE YOUR NEED FOR SPIRITUAL ASSISTANCE

In his best courtroom style, Dale passionately defended the lies of the Messiah Trap, "I disagree with you on this point. I believe

that I *am* responsible for the welfare of those around me, for doing something about the injustice I see."

Like Dale, Messiahs fall prey to the Trap because its lies contain
partial truths. Yes, as members of the human community we are
responsible to each other—for treating each other with dignity,
protecting those more vulnerable, and helping those in need.
The Messiah Trap errs, however, in the *degree* to which it over-
states our responsibility (Side 1) and understates our worth
(Side 2).

As I have struggled to let go of the first side of the Messiah
Trap, I have often been hindered by my fear of what would happen if I stopped playing the Messiah. For the tremendous sense of
responsibility that I carried, one would suppose that the entire
human race would suffer an alteration in the cosmic order when I
started "letting go." Much to my relief (and also to my dismay, I
must admit), no such intergalactic trauma was experienced. My
relinquishment of my Messiah duties wasn't even covered on the
local news. (*You* didn't notice, did you?) The impact was felt primarily in my own life as the chains of the Messiah Trap began to
crack away from my hands and heart.

The fact of the matter is, we are not indispensable. Sorry.

"But they need me!" Dale insisted, momentarily losing his com-
posure as tears welled up in his eyes. I understood Dale's pain as it
burst through his well-trained defense. I have never experienced
greater suffering than that resulting from facing my own limitations. No other loss or violation has been comparable. What can
be more distressful than to give everything one has in the care for
others only to realize that the sacrifice is insufficient? Have Messiahs not suffered by receiving a call from the emergency room
saying that a client finally succeeded in committing suicide? Do
Messiahs not wrestle in sleepless beds over vulnerable children
who suffer abuse inflicted on them by their parents and "the system"? How can one be comforted when famine spreads despite
efforts at hunger relief and the threat of nuclear war escalates in
the face of dedicated peace work? Continually confronted with
human limitations, Messiahs are cruelly teased by the Messiah
Trap because it offers false hope in one's own power. Messiahs do
not have the ability to save other people.

It is time to stop this pretense, time to grieve for all the children, the elderly, the sick, the hungry, the homeless, the needy we

will never be able to save. Messiahs cannot keep fathers from drinking, mothers from contracting breast cancer, brothers from dying in wars, sisters from being raped, or children from abusing drugs. We simply do not have the power.

Not only do we not have the power to save other people, we do not even have the power to save ourselves. When we were children, we were not able to protect ourselves from violation. As we grew older, we did not save ourselves from falling prey to the lies of the Messiah Trap. Messiahs are as vulnerable as anyone else to the threat of violence, war, illness, mental distress, loss, and loneliness. Pretending to be powerful does not make one so.

If the false hope offered by the Messiah Trap is rejected, is one left without any hope at all?

"I'm really frightened," Dale looked at me with childlike eyes. "I never realized that letting go of the Messiah Trap would be so painful. I don't have the power to deal with all this on my own." He stood up and wandered to the window. Jamming his hands deep into his pockets, he leaned against the wall and stared outside like a little boy waiting for someone to come and take him home. "I'm embarrassed to say this but whenever I'm alone I find myself trying to talk to God. I haven't prayed since I was a little boy. It seems so . . . so, I don't know, so silly somehow."

"I don't find it silly at all," I responded. "We all come to moments in our lives when we realize we are not big enough or strong enough to make it through." In my mind I recalled the nights where the despair was so thick no human hand could comfort me. But I remembered the passages in Psalms that did touch my heart, such as "Be still and know that I am God" and "In my anguish I cried to the Lord and He answered by setting me free." I confided to Dale, "I have faced such moments as you are facing now, Dale, and I've found that I am not alone. God has been with me."

A wave of peace flowed over Dale's face. "Yes. I've felt that too. I was just afraid to trust that God was really there for me." A fragile smile played around his mouth. "Do you mean I don't have to pretend I'm in control of the world any more?"

I smiled back in affirmation.

Dale's face broke into a full grin as he teased, "After you've played God, what do you do for an encore?"

I chuckled. "You're free to write your own script now, Dale. You're breaking free."

2. COOPERATE WITH THE PROCESS OF GROWTH

The woman sitting before me barely resembled the Elizabeth I had met several months before. Stringy red hair hung over her eyes. She whispered quietly, "I've done everything I know how to do, and it's just not enough. I feel so overwhelmed, so defeated." She stared off across the room at a scene I could not see. "I keep having this impulse to run away to some quiet place and hide."

"What keeps you from doing that, Elizabeth?" I asked softly.

Her face twisted toward me with a look of surprise. "You want me to run away? I've got all these responsibilities and so much to do." Dragging her tired hands through her hair she despaired, "I wish someone would tell me what to do. I'm so confused and all out of answers."

"You know exactly what to do, Elizabeth," I responded firmly. "You have just told yourself what to do next."

Crinkling her face up in frustration, she snapped, "Don't play games with me. I just told you I was confused."

"What you have just told me," I pressed, "is that you have received a message from your inner self telling you to stop playing the Messiah. It's time to stop pretending that you are indispensable. Your impulse to be alone and quiet is guidance from yourself. Trust yourself, Elizabeth. Listen."

As we sat together in silence, I reflected on the choices I had made in my journey as well as on those made by other friends and clients. Granted, at times there seem to be more problems than answers, more pain than comfort, and more confusion than clarity of vision. Yet in the middle of the competing voices and conflicting advice, I have come to recognize an inner message that points us toward our next step. In order to understand and properly respond to this message, it is crucial to recognize its origin.

Since we were created by a Being who desires relationship with us, it is not surprising to discover that we long for intimacy with others, ourselves, and God. We all experience varying degrees of alienation and separation. Many people in our society today are so separated from their spiritual selves that they deny, not only the existence of God, but the existence of the spiritual realm altogether. Many others acknowledge some aspect of their spiritual selves but become lost in philosophical frameworks that strip the spirit of personhood. These people define God as an energy force or extension of a purely mechanistic, naturalistic universe. I have found repeatedly in my own life and in the lives of friends and clients that if we listen to our deeper selves, to the small voice within us, we are led slowly but surely back to an experience of healing and into a deeper relationship with ourselves and with a personal Being who loves us. We are not merely being teased or misguided by this longing for intimacy and wholeness but are being directed toward reunion. It is a direction that we can trust because God is trustworthy. Our task is to cooperate with the growth by listening and responding to the messages provided.

These messages may come in a variety of ways. Sometimes we are signaled by way of a dream or through a visualization during meditation. Some people feel a "leading" through prayer or scripture reading. Others experience flashes of insight in therapy.

Many times, however, we overlook these messages due to our lack of trust in ourselves and the process of growth. The general society and even many Christian circles limit truth to that which can be discerned through logical and rationalistic thought forms. Consequently, these people miss the messages God sends to them each day through images, impulses, and feelings. They ignore the messages sent each night when they dream—images of hope, problem clarification, or direction.

Another way people do not cooperate with the process of growth is by misinterpreting the messages received from God and from the inner self. Since our unconscious minds are attempting to signal us, it is not uncommon for messages to be attached to activities or experiences that will get our attention. An example is the husband who finds himself intensely attracted to another woman. She seems to bring him alive with desire, with a fantasy of sexual and emotional intimacy. He may give way to this impulse by initiating an affair or he may try to push this forbidden desire away. Taking either of these two choices illustrates that this man is misinterpreting his inner message, which is drawing him to look inside himself. He may be called to address a variety of issues. He may need to enlarge his capacity to take in nurturance, to explore unresolved pain in his childhood, to raise the level of intimacy within his marriage, or to address conflict with his inner feminine self. If he misinterprets the message by acting out the impulse and having an affair or by repressing it, the message will simply be re-coded and sent to him again—this time attached to another impulse. Needs for healing and growth do not go away simply because they are ignored, misinterpreted, or neglected. We will be at peace only after we have accurately received and cooperated with the call to growth.

In Elizabeth's situation, her needs for spiritual and emotional growth had been neglected by getting caught up in the frantic pace of the Messiah Trap. She misinterpreted her urge to run away to a secluded place as a forbidden impulse to be resisted— when she was actually being called to rest, to listen, and to open herself up to intimacy. Elizabeth needed no new insight or direction. She merely needed to listen to her inner voice and to respond to the guidance she was being given. Her next step was to trust herself, trust the process of growth, and to trust the Author of growth.

3. ATTEND TO YOUR INNER WORK

"What you are suggesting could alter the entire course of my life," James said solemnly, fists clamped tightly together. "My whole life is built around helping other people." He desired freedom from a lifestyle that had left him physically damaged and emotionally estranged from others. And yet James was fearful of letting go of being a Messiah because that was the only way he knew to live his life.

James had spent many years in college training to be a Messiah. The woman he chose to marry was also a Messiah, and together they constructed a lifestyle wherein they neglected their own needs and overinvested themselves in the lives of others. James was admired for the sacrifices he had made and had received many awards and honors. One could even say that his very livelihood depended on his capacity to perform as a Messiah. It takes a great deal of courage to re-examine the very foundation of one's life—a great deal of courage. Fortunately, James was a man of courage.

"Suppose I did release my exaggerated sense of responsibility for other people," James ventured cautiously, "What next? This is all I know how to do. What would I do instead? I'm afraid if I change, I'll feel useless and worthless."

As James began to break away from the first side the Messiah Trap by releasing a sense of responsibility for others, the second side was close behind to trip him. The second side of the Messiah Trap is the lie of earned worth—wherein he was told that he was not intrinsically valuable but that his worth could be earned by his behavior (by "playing God"). I believe that all human beings have intrinsic worth because we have been created by God, who is the source of all that is valuable. We do not increase our value when we make other people happy, gain people's trust, or provide them with the things they need. Messiahs do not move up a notch on the "worth" scale by giving to the poor, protecting the vulnerable, or rescuing those in crisis. Studying and grappling with complicated issues may increase understanding, but these efforts add nothing to a person's value. The causes for which you fight may be worthy, but they do not increase your worth.

The reason you cannot earn your worth is because you are already worthy. All you can do is accept what is already yours. This may sound too easy, especially when compared to the enormous tasks Messiahs have previously taken on. Messiahs are accustomed to leaping tall problems in a single bound, racing from client to client faster than a speeding bullet. Do not be fooled by the simplicity of the task. Since Messiahs are used to working passionately toward a desired goal, it can be quite disorienting to find you are already there.

"Would you say you are a passive or active person?" I asked James.

"I'm definitely an active person," he responded emphatically. "I'm always on the go. There's so much to do."

"Then I would suggest that you try the opposite for a while," I said. "Whenever you feel like you need to do something, I'd like you to sit down, wait, and listen."

James looked at me as if I had lost my mind. "You want me to sit around and do nothing? I'd feel absolutely useless!"

When not overly involved in helping others, Messiahs tend to feel worthless and helpless. To combat these feelings, Messiahs tend to throw themselves back into a flurry of activity by launching new campaigns, counseling with new vigor, giving with more sacrifice, and speaking out with new conviction. Messiahs do and do and then do some more. While you may eventually be able to help others in a balanced way, in the initial phase of letting go of the Messiah Trap I strongly recommend that you try to resist any urge you may have to please, rescue, give, protect, counsel, teach, or crusade. In order to let go of the Messiah Trap, you must first learn to wait, be still, and listen.

"I am not suggesting that you are to be inactive," I told James. "Learning to listen and respond to your inner self is anything but inactive, and it is certainly not easy."

Messiahs tend to be quite adept at maneuvering in the external world and equally unskilled at navigating in the inner regions. Although Messiahs often neglect their inner journeys, there is an intimate interplay between the inner and outer worlds, both affecting each other. As you release your hold on the Messiah Trap, it becomes increasingly important to develop an understanding of these two realms, especially when you are attempting to acknowledge and address your own needs and growth. The point I would like to stress is this: *Inner issues must be addressed on an inner level, and outer issues must be addressed on an outer level.*

This point may seem rather obvious, yet Messiahs rarely act as if they understand this principle at all. When faced with an inner issue (childhood hurts or feelings of helplessness, for example), Messiahs almost always attempt to resolve the problem in the outer realm and neglect the inner work required. For the most part, Messiahs try to deal with inner issues through external accomplishments. In an effort to acquire a sense of worth, which is an inner issue, Messiahs tend to become involved in a variety of external activities such as earning college degrees, landing prestigious jobs, making speeches to large crowds, talking someone through a crisis, writing, giving away possessions, and fulfilling every request people may make. When holding fast to the Messiah Trap, one is blinded to the fact that, since the pain is within, attempts at resolution in the external realm are futile. The Messiah Trap enslaves you to an outward journey that leads nowhere. You can experience inner healing and growth only once you are launched on the journey inward.

Throughout history, people of all backgrounds have discovered the joys, toils, and rewards of inner work. This process has acquired a number of names over the years: *prayer, meditation, contemplation, reflection.* This inner work may include journal writing, dream analysis, active imagination, painting, song or poetry writing, or other art forms. You may journey into your inner realm as you take long walks in the woods or through city streets. You may journey alone or with the help of a therapist or support group.

When attending to your inner work, you have the opportunity to get to know yourself in a way you may never have before. The Messiah Trap has kept you from knowing yourself accurately because it has told you lies about yourself. The Messiah Trap draws you into a frustrating whirlwind of disappointment. You are told you are guilty when you are innocent, tied down when you are free, and last in line when it is your turn. It is time to honestly face yourself in the silence.

"When I came into counseling, I never expected to find that hiding behind my ulcer was the Messiah Trap," James said, and smiled wryly. "And I didn't expect it to be so frightening. You would think I'd feel relieved to find that, while I am to help others, it is not my sole responsibility to 'save' them. You would also think it'd be good news to learn that I am a valuable person regardless of what I accomplish. Instead I feel somewhat disoriented." He sighed deeply.

"I think it is finally time for me to get off this treadmill, turn down the volume in my life, and listen to myself and to God before I act." Glancing out the window, he said thoughtfully, "I wonder what I will hear."

4. LISTEN TO THE HURTING CHILD INSIDE

In nearly every session, Alicia cried. There had been tears for the starving children in Africa that Alicia wished she could have saved. She had wept over what she could not give her own children. For months Alicia had agonized over the troubles of her sister, her mother, her father.

Today, Alicia was crying again, only these tears were different. Tremors of sorrow broke loose from deep inside her. As the pain of her childhood burst through the thick walls she had constructed, her body began to shake. Alicia was finally crying her own tears. She was crying for herself.

At first her agony was too deep for words as she shook with silent sobs. Finding her voice, the room filled with a moaning that at once expressed her sadness and her fear. With her eyes squeezed shut, she whispered between sobs, "They never really cared about me . . . only used me . . . I never really was special . . . all I wanted was to be loved."

The pretending was over for Alicia. She was no longer ignoring the cries of the little girl inside her, that part of her that had been so deeply wounded. Slowly Alicia leaned back heavily on the cushions of the couch. She wiped her face with a tissue and began to explore the source of her sorrow. "I keep hoping that my parents will notice me, realize I still need their love, but they never do. Everything I give them, I wish they would give to me. I feel so empty."

Like Alicia, we must learn to listen to ourselves if we ever hope to break free of the Messiah Trap. Many people resist being quiet and listening for their "inner child" because of their fear of what they might hear. You may very likely hear crying. By allowing your inner child to take you back in time and honestly examine your childhood, you may have to acknowledge disappointments and losses, violation and deprivation, deficits and unmet needs. You may need to grieve a childhood lost.

"There are times," Alicia told me, "when I feel like I never was a child. It seems like I've been taking care of everyone else ever since I can remember. I helped my brothers and sister get dressed in the morning, did the housework to protect my mother and please my dad." Alicia dug her fist into a pillow. "It really makes me angry when I face the fact that no one was there to take care of me."

Alicia paused and dropped her head. "What are you feeling?" I asked her. "Are you feeling guilty over your anger?"

She nodded. "After all, they did give me a place to live and we did have some good times." Looking up at me, she continued, "I think I'm afraid to get angry. I'm afraid I'll hurt someone the way my dad did when he got mad."

As you come to realize what the Messiah Trap has cost you, it is common to experience anger in an intense and frightening degree. This anger may hit in stages as you more deeply acknowledge the damage you may have suffered—the loss of parts of your childhood, the lies you were told about your worth, the opportunities for intimacy missed, and the years lost to futile Messiah endeavors.

As you discard the Messiah Trap, I suggest that you explore your anger gradually and with the assistance of a counselor. Anger is an emotion full of energy. This energy can be harnessed for healing or destruction. If released inappropriately, anger can wreak a tremendous amount of damage in our own lives and certainly on those who are the recipients of our rage. Anger is an emotion to be addressed slowly and with respect for its potential violence. These are a few outlets that have worked for my clients, my friends, and myself:

- Talking to a friend or therapist
- Taking a walk
- Hitting a pillow (*never* hitting a living being)
- Yelling in a room or a car by yourself
- Writing in a journal
- Engaging in physical exercise such as lifting weights, jogging, or playing racquet ball or tennis
- Crying
- Praying
- Painting

I believe that anger is intended to serve as a signal to us that we are being violated. It is proper to be angry when mistreated and it can be productive to use that energy to protect ourselves from danger. If we listen to anger's messages when we first received them, we are more likely to protect ourselves from damage and are more able to express feelings appropriately.

"What are some of the ways you express your anger?" I asked Alicia.

"I talk to you," she responded. "You don't seem to be afraid of my anger, and that helps me." She paused. "The other night I wrote this awful letter to my father, telling him all the things I wish I could say, and then tore it up and threw the piece around the room. I felt better after that."

"Did you consider mailing that letter to your father?" I inquired.

"No, I'm not ready for that." Alicia pulled further away from me.

I studied her for a moment. "You're not fully convinced that you deserve to be treated well, are you?"

Once again she began to cry. "There's still a part of me that says I deserved what I got."

Softly I said, "What you deserved, Alicia, was to be loved."

5. IDENTIFY YOUR OWN NEEDS AND WANTS

All Messiahs have needs because all human beings have needs and, contrary to common self-deception. *Messiahs are human beings.* We Messiahs have gone to great lengths to hide a sense of neediness from others and especially from ourselves. Messiahs have even pretended to be unlike other people, to be different, to be *Messiahs!* Once we relinquish the Messiah Trap, we have the opportunity to identify our legitimate needs and wants.

Identifying what you need and want may be more difficult than you imagine. By getting caught up in meeting the needs of others and giving them what *they* seem to want, you probably have spent little time listening to yourself. In fact, you may never have developed the skills necessary to identify your needs and wants. Try asking yourself what you want. Does the answer to that question come readily? Or do you find yourself fumbling a bit, looking to someone else for direction?

The perplexed expression on Diedre's face indicated that she was having trouble answering that same question. "What do I want?" she repeated, "Well, if I knew the answer to that, I wouldn't be in counseling now! I have spent my childhood pleasing my parents, my married life taking care of my husband and children, and my professional life nurturing my clients."

"For the moment, let go of all those obligations and constraints, and contemplate what you need. What do you want out of life, Diedre? What are the things you like to do? What do you want?" I asked.

Diedre stared up in amazement, "You know, I don't think anyone has ever asked me that before. People ask me to listen to them and to give them what they want, but I don't think anyone has ever really wanted to know what's going on inside of me." She paused for a moment, "And now that I am faced with the question, I have to admit that I haven't the slightest idea how to answer."

Diedre's quandary is very common among recovering Messiahs. Messiahs, although often very dynamic and opinionated people, have spent little time developing personal tastes or interests. Messiahs often buy clothes that please others, decorate their homes in line with the tastes of friends, and if they take vacations, they engage in activities that provide some service to someone else (such as visiting relatives or attending out-of-town conferences and calling it a vacation). Do *you* know what *you* like? want? need? When experiencing difficulty in discerning your own needs, it may be helpful to begin by observing what you provide for others. Often we give to other people what we unconsciously know that we need ourselves.

Are you a Pleaser? Perhaps you are in need of emotional care and it is time you attended to your own sense of well-being. You have long attended to the happiness of others. It may be time now to focus on your own sense of happiness.

If you are a Giver, perhaps you are in need of more tangible nurturance. How would you spend your money if you didn't feel obligated to give it all away? What are the things you have wanted but felt too guilty to buy? It may be time to learn how to nurture yourself through giftgiving, as you once exclusively nurtured others in the past.

Protectors and Rescuers are often people who have inner fears and special vulnerabilities. Is there someone you need to confront, someone that has intruded on you? Do you need to defend your own personal space or protect yourself from danger? Perhaps it is time to learn to be more assertive and discerning, to use the support of others as you better protect yourself from exploitation.

Counselors are often hungry for intimacy, comfort, and support. This may be a time when you need to open yourself up to personal relationships in new ways—either by initiation new friendships or deepening the relationships with those in your life. You may need someone to listen to you tell your story. You may need to learn to trust and risk.

Are you a Teacher? Perhaps you have a deep need for attention and affection. Is now the time to get off the stage and approach others in a more intimate manner? Is there a talent or interest you have that you have neglected because of the time you've spent in Messiah activities? Perhaps attention should be paid to these areas, which can provide you with another source of reward and sense of accomplishment.

If you are a Crusader, you may need to be your own advocate and fight for your own cause. What injustices have you been subjected to? Perhaps it's time to take a stand in your own behalf.

As Messiahs, our needs are many and we deserve the time and energy it requires to listen to and attend to ourselves. It is time for us to break free of our overly serious approach to life and laugh, have fun, cultivate frivolity, and joy. We Messiahs need to learn how to say "Yes!"—to having fun, to going on adventures, to attending spiritual retreats, to spontaneous outings, to developing our artistic talents, to listening to music, to reading enjoyable books, to soaking in bubble baths, to exercising regularly, to filling our homes with cut flowers and beauty and art. When we say "yes" to our needs and wants, we will find ourselves enjoying our children, communicating better with spouses, laughing more with friends. There may be projects to begin, such as building a boat, sewing an outfit, or learning gourmet cooking. There may be short stories to write, paintings to paint, or music to play. The Messiah Trap has been a barrier to so many important and enjoyable experiences. It is time to let go of the Messiah Trap and say "Yes!" to these opportunities.

"This is great in theory," Diedre pointed out with skepticism, "but when do you think I'm going to find the time for all these activities? I've got responsibilities and obligations, I can't just run off whenever the mood hits me."

"Well, there is one little hitch," I smiled. "You can't learn how to say 'Yes!' until you learn how to say 'No!' "

When you let go of the Messiah Trap, you also let go of the pretense that you are a limitless source of nurturance for others. Since so many Messiahs are overextended and overinvested, most need to back up, cut back, say "No!" This may entail cutting back on the number of clients you see, committees on which you will serve, nights you take work home from the office, weekends you spend out of town on business. This may involve redefining relationships within families and social circles. You may even be faced with the necessity of ending some relationships. This process is what I refer to as "pruning."

Pruning requires saying "No!"—a word that is very hard for Messiahs to say. While all aspects of growth and healing are difficult for Messiahs to face, the pruning process seems one of the most troublesome. It is, however, inescapable if you are to be free of the Messiah Trap. When you say "No!" you stand nose to nose with the lies of the Messiah Trap, contradicting the lies that have held you captive for so long. You reject Side 1 by saying "Sorry, this is not my responsibility. If that is going to get done, someone else will have to take responsibility for it." You contradict Side 2 when you say "No!" You declare your worth by clearly stating, "*My* needs take priority at this time."

Do you want to know how free you are from the Messiah Trap? The answer, in part, lies in how well you are able to say "No!" When you are able to set a life structure that enhances growth and facilitates intimacy, you are well on your way to freedom.

"If being able to say 'No!' is an indicator of my success," Diedre confided, "then I'm not doing so well. Just yesterday, for example, I gave a presentation at a conference. Late in the evening, when I was trying to leave, a woman came up to me and asked to speak with me. I told her it was late and offered her my card but she said it wouldn't take very long, that my presentation had really hit home for her. She went on to say that she'd never tried to talk to anyone else about this before but my presentation gave her the hope that she could trust me."

"I then told her we could talk if she wanted to walk me to my car. She seemed grateful and began to tell me how frightened she was, that she needed help desperately, and was scared of what she might do to herself." Diedre leaned back and sighed in defeat. "I ended up taking her out for coffee and we talked till after midnight."

Like Diedre, Messiahs expect to carry more than their share and are, therefore, easily manipulated into taking care of others. It may be difficult to admit just how susceptible we are to these manipulations, since we pride ourselves in being strong, not weak; wise, not foolish. If you take an honest look at your behavior, however, you may find that you often do what other people want you to do, whether you want to or not. Do you say "yes" to their requests when you need to say "no"? Perhaps you really do believe that other people are inadequate, that they need you and that they need you now.

As Diedre and I examined her experience at the conference, it became clear how the Messiah Trap was set for her. The woman requesting help told her that Diedre appeared to be the only person who could help her (Side 1). In insinuating that she was suicidal, she placed her needs over Diedre's (Side 2). People manipulate Messiahs by putting bait on the Messiah Trap. They present problems and situations in which it appears that only a Messiah can save them and that seem to warrant immediate attention. Each of the seven Messiah styles are susceptible to different kinds of bait:

1. The Pleaser is susceptible to those who appear dependent and unhappy.
2. The Giver is susceptible to those who appear in need.
3. The Protector is susceptible to those who appear inadequate and in danger.
4. The Rescuer is susceptible to those who appear incompetent and in crisis.
5. The Counselor is susceptible to those who appear confused and troubled.
6. The Teacher is susceptible to those who appear to be searching for truth and for a hero..
7. The Crusader is susceptible to those who appear unjustly treated.

When Messiahs overestimate their power, they also underestimate the resourcefulness of others. But how can we doubt their resourcefulness if we step back for a moment and see what they can get Messiahs to do? At their bidding, Messiahs give away material possessions, emotional resources, and spiritual insights. It came as quite a shock to me to find that when I did not, for whatever reason, meet the needs of others, they did not fall apart. Instead, they turned to someone else! They simply found another Messiah to take care of them.

Perhaps this is one reason it is so hard for Messiahs to say "No!" It is not that we feel so indispensable as we claim, but are afraid that if we don't respond as expected, we will be easily replaced. Messiahs want to feel special, to feel that those we help really need *us*—not just anybody—we want them to need us in particular.

"So you are suggesting that the reason I stayed up late with that woman was not so much that she really needed me but that I needed her to need me?" Diedre asked.

"If you felt she was pushing you past reasonable limits, what could you have done to help her without falling into the Messiah Trap?" I responded.

Diedre thought for a moment. "I suppose I could have made an appointment with her during office hours," she said.

I agreed. "That way you would have offered her assistance but communicated your limitations as well. What could you have done to address the threat of suicide?"

Diedre answered, "Given her the number to the counseling center hotline or even called for assistance if I really thought she was a danger to herself. I guess there were several ways I could have helped without playing the Messiah. She seemed like she was in so much pain, I just didn't want to make her feel rejected."

Messiahs often resist saying "no" in an effort to protect others from pain and from their legitimate suffering. Suffering is an experience most have tried to avoid because the role of pain is misunderstood. In our society, suffering is often viewed as something unusual, unnecessary, and certainly unfair. Television commercials promise the "good life" full of sensual pleasure and waiting to be bought at the store. Family crises are resolved in thirty-minute segments, criminals captured and convicted in an hour. According to this distortion, life is supposed to be pain-free.

Messiahs often hold onto the Messiah Trap in the mistaken belief that suffering is thereby avoided. As Messiahs, we have intended to put an end to the world's trauma and pain. The problem with the attempt to avoid pain through the Messiah Trap is simple—it doesn't work. Not only is pain *not* avoided, but the negative impact on ourselves and others is also often compounded and intensified by Messiah actions. *We do not avoid suffering by playing Messiah. We do, however, avoid growth and intimacy.*

The Messiah does no one a favor by standing between others and their pain. Doing so interferes with the process of growth. Messiah interventions often block the natural consequences of choice. As long as a Messiah is around to buffer the impact of one's poor choice, the consequences of one's own behavior can never be learned. People often learn that they do not have to be responsible for their own growth because Messiahs relieve them of that duty. The Messiah may sacrifice personal growth for others, only to succeed in blocking their growth as well. You make gains, not for yourself or those you may attempt to help, when holding onto the Messiah Trap.

When you make choices for your own growth, however, you also make opportunities for others to grow as well. When you speak the truth, whether or not it is pleasing, you allow others the choice to accept reality or push it away. By accepting the pain that accompanies growth in your own life, you will be less likely to try to rescue others from their legitimate suffering. The prospect of pain is less likely to deter you from growth because it no longer holds the terror it may have once had. You have the opportunity to trade fear, confusion, panic, and weakness for courage, endurance, patience, and strength. By saying "No!" to the Messiah Trap, you allow others to take responsibility for their own lives and for the development of their own self-esteem.

It is important to note that the difference between damaging someone and displeasing them. This differentiation Messiahs seem unable to make. We believe that if we inconvenience someone, refuse a request, or tell another person something they may be unwilling to hear, they are in some way *damaged.* This is not the case. What we are doing is simply inconveniencing someone, refusing a request, or telling them something they may not be willing to hear. No more. No less. As you let go of your Messiah role, people may respond as if you had committed some dastardly deed, inflicted some irreparable destruction on their lives. But what you have really done is place on their shoulders the responsibility for their own lives—where it belongs. This sets you free to take responsibility for yourself, for your own mistakes, and for your own growth.

6. ACKNOWLEDGE THE DAMAGE YOU HAVE DONE TO OTHERS

While there were just a few feet between Cindi and Paul as they sat at opposite ends of the couch, the gulf between them seemed unbridgeable. Cindi clung bitterly to the hurt she had suffered from Paul's Messiah actions while Paul relentlessly defended his actions as noble, even as godly.

"Cindi, what about Paul attracted you when you first met?" I asked.

Cindi inhaled deeply. "Oh, that was so long ago," she sighed.

"When I met Paul, I was still living at home. There was always so much fighting at my house, but at Paul's it was always calm." Cindi looked over at Paul for the first time during the session. "I guess I felt secure with Paul. He was so kind and always took care of me. Once he even stood up to my dad."

"So you were originally drawn to Paul's protective behavior?" I asked.

Cindi sighed again. "Yes, I suppose so. I was a little girl then. The problem is that I'm not a little girl anymore." Turning toward Paul, she said softly, "Can't you see that I am a woman now? I don't need you to protect me."

Rubbing his forehead, Paul looked back at her fearfully. "I'm afraid that you don't need me at all," he said.

Cindi stared at the floor in silence.

Turning to me, he confessed, "I can see how I have hurt Cindi. I have fooled myself into thinking that I am protecting Cindi from harm. But I'm afraid to give that up. What if she finds out that she can do everything on her own and she doesn't need me anymore?"

I urged Paul to ask Cindi what she needed. Cautiously moving closer to his wife, he asked, "Cindi, is there anything you need from me?"

"I don't need to be caged or controlled by you," she responded. "I need you to apologize for how you've hurt me."

"I really am sorry—" His voice broke. Beginning again, he said, "I really am sorry for hurting you. I never intended to hurt you, but I can see that I have."

Facing the hurt we have caused others can be as difficult as facing the pain we have suffered at the hands of others. All Messiahs have hurt others through Messiah behaviors. It may be tempting to deny this, unfortunately it is true. Each Messiah style tends to hurt others in a different manner:

- *Pleasers:* Pleasers tend to cut others off because Pleasers hide their feelings behind the pretense of trying to please.
- *Protectors:* Like the Pleaser, Protectors hurt others by distorting and manipulating the truth. By pretending to protect others, Messiahs actually put themselves into positions of control and power.
- *Givers:* Although Givers want to see themselves as people concerned about the welfare of others, they use the act of giving as a way to control others. People are kept at a distance as the

Giver forces gifts on others but refuses to accept their expressions of caring.

- *Rescuers:* While fooled into thinking they are invaluable in a crisis, Rescuers actually reinforce the feelings of helplessness in others. The self-esteem of others is sacrificed to the Messiah's feeling of being powerful and strong.
- *Counselors:* Mutual intimacy is most difficult for Counselors, and yet needed desperately. Consequently, others are drawn to a point where they are intimate and vulnerable, while the Counselor hides behind the Counselor role. Others are hurt by the Counselor's refusing to provide mutual intimacy and keeping them in a less powerful, more vulnerable role.
- *Teachers:* Teachers avoid mutual intimacy by hiding in the crowd, by cultivating the admiration of others, and yet by not returning that caring on a mutual basis. Others are left feeling untouched and unloved, frustrated by the invisible barrier between the Teacher and those who need intimacy and nurturance.
- *Crusaders:* Dedicated Crusaders view others more as objects than as human beings. Each person becomes an ally or an enemy, a co-worker or an obstacle, someone to take care of or someone to help in the cause. Crusaders appear to be deeply caring human beings and yet leave others alone in their feelings, cut off from the Crusader's inner self.

It is critical (though painful) to acknowledge the damage he or she has inflicted on others if the Messiah is to let go of the Messiah Trap and if *real* healing and growth is to be facilitated in the lives of those the Messiah touches. It is a humbling experience—one that Messiahs try to avoid by "playing god." But by facing yourself and your failings honestly, you can at last open the door to genuine reconciliation and intimacy.

"What do you need from Cindi?" I asked Paul.

Struggling with his feelings, Paul answered, "I need some hope that we can work this out." Picking up his wife's hand, he continued, "Cindi, you know how hard this is for me to say. I always try to be the strong one, but I want you to know that I need you. I need you to forgive me, and I need you to stay."

With tears in her eyes, Cindi squeezed his hand and nodded.

7. LEARN TO ACCEPT LOVE AND NURTURANCE

Gary stared out the window for such a long time I wondered if he had heard my question. "Do you have anyone you talk to about your feelings?" I repeated.

He turned and smiled sadly. "I heard you. I was trying to think of someone. I have acquaintances and business associates, and certainly plenty of students, but no one I would call for help. There's no one I really open up to."

He pinched his eyebrows together as he searched his mind for someone he could trust. "Now that I think about this, I can see that I never talk about what's going on with me. All the conversations I have revolve around someone else's problems and, once their problem is taken care of, I don't seem to have much to say."

Messiahs do one thing extremely well—help. If helping is all we feel comfortable doing, what do we do with a person who has no problem? How do we act? If we can feel good about ourselves only when people look up to us, what do we do with a person who doesn't want our advice? What do we talk about? And if we only know how to establish relationships with people who need us, where do we go when we need help? How do we ask for help? To whom can we turn?

Gary turned his head back toward the window. "As long as I keep busy, keep the noise level full blast, I can get by. But when I stop," he whispered, "I feel so alone. Sometimes I feel so needy it terrifies me."

I suspect that one reason why Messiahs are reluctant to acknowledge their own neediness is that they have long ago discarded the hope that these needs will be met. Why uncover loneliness, vulnerabilities, and desires if the pain will merely be increased through exposure but no satisfaction will be available? It is much safer to pretend there are no needs inside, no longings for intimacy, no pain throbbing deep within.

As I have talked with friends and clients struggling to let go of the Messiah Trap, I have often heard the complaint that they do not have access to the things or relationships that would satisfy them. There have been descriptions of intense loneliness, followed by the claim that there was no one in their lives who loved them. If they were married, they did not feel their spouses loved them enough. Those who were single were certain that their pain was due to their unmarried state. The loneliness felt was defined as the absence of love and a great deal of energy went into "finding" that love.

I believe that Messiahs are emotionally undernourished, not because the banquet is sparse, but because Messiahs have tiny little mouths that are incapable of taking in the feast. A person's longings do not indicate what life has to offer. On the contrary, the level of need indicates what portions of life that person is currently capable of experiencing. In all my professional and personal observation, I have never met a person who was capable of accepting more love and nurturance than he or she was currently experiencing. Should a new relationship or affair seem to promise more, it was not long before the aura faded, the relationship proved disappointing, and the person felt lonely again.

It has been illustrated that we are capable of loving others to the extent that we have received love. Studies have shown that infants who are neglected, and who do not bond with a parent or caretaker, often become detached and unresponsive. As adults, these people have great difficulty in establishing warm relationships. All of us are truly vulnerable in this regard. We are totally dependent on someone else loving us for us to be able to love back.

The Christian message speaks to this profound dependency by telling us that God loved us *first*. When we were unlovable and unable to love, God loved us and initiated our capacity to love in response. This spiritual reality permeates our relationships. Even those of us who have been entangled in the Messiah Trap have all been nourished by love, somewhere, sometime, by someone. We may have enjoyed the love of our parents, of siblings, and other family members. We may have had friends along the way who have shown us glimpses of loving that increased our ability to love again. Regardless of our capacity to receive love, we have been offered love throughout our lives.

"Who is offering you love at the present time?" I asked Gary.

"Well," he hesitated, "I suppose you are. You listen to me and seem to understand. You haven't condemned me for all my failings."

"Perhaps this relationship is a place to start, then," I suggested. "As you are more able to accept the nurturance in our relationship, more able to trust, you will be more able to risk intimacy in your personal life. Maybe with Annie."

Gary sighed heavily, "It seems like such a tiny step, too tiny. Trusting you is one thing. Trusting Annie again seems impossible. I wonder if I have the patience."

The process of growth does require patience, for it is a journey.

You will not "arrive" one day at a destination or be pronounced "cured." Instead, this journey is a series of choices. The lies of the Messiah Trap may have caused you to doubt your worth and to limit your ability to be in a relationship. As the Messiah Trap is released, you are presented with a choice—you can open yourself up to the love that currently exists in your life or close off telling yourself there is no one out there who cares. You can accept the truth or hold fast to the lies.

This choice is made, between truth and deception, many times a day—sometimes in dramatic ways but most often in quiet, almost hidden ways. Do you believe the lies of the Messiah Trap and conclude that you must earn the love you receive? Consequently, do you find yourself feeling trapped within a relationship where you do all the giving and the other person does all the taking? If asked to take on an additional helping activity that will conflict with a family outing, do you sacrifice intimacy with your family (holding fast to the Messiah Trap), or do you protect precious time with your spouse and children? When a family member asks for attention during a time reserved for personal meditation, do you make the choice to protect or neglect your own need for inner nurturance?

When you say "no" to the Messiah Trap and "yes" to growth and intimacy, you are choosing love—and when you choose love, you also increase your capacity to give and receive love. When you sacrifice your growth and opportunities for intimacy, you rechain yourself to the Messiah Trap. Although these choices may seem small, we are continually provided with opportunities to take our next tiny step away from or toward our healing.

Once this process is understood and accepted, attention becomes focused where it belongs—on increasing our capacity to accept love and to return love, no longer trying to "track it down" as if love were something trying to elude us. We can concentrate on cooperating with the process of growth and opening our eyes to the fact that in each of our lives, at the present time, there exist more opportunities for nurturance, joy, intimacy, and love than we are currently able to enjoy. Free of the Messiah Trap, we are faced with the challenge of learning to receive, learning to trust, learning to share, learning to take nurturance from love as it is. *Love, as it is, is enough.*

Appendix A: How to Find the Help You Need

INDIVIDUAL COUNSELING

Perhaps one of the most troublesome tasks facing the escaping Messiah is trying to find someone who can help. Bobbing on the turbulent waters of newly identified emotions, Messiahs often need the structure, protection, and guidance provided by trained psychotherapists and spiritual directors. It is critical that the person selected to help *not* be a practicing Messiah. Often it is difficult to find a counselor because some of the people drawn to such activities are themselves Messiah Counselors. A Messiah Counselor will not understand your reason for being in counseling because he or she will not have insight into why he or she is in the role of counselor. Should a Messiah Counselor catch a glimpse of what you are struggling with, the result may be one of insult or sabotage. You may find yourself unintentionally exposing the issues of the Counselor and possibly rendering your therapeutic relationship useless.

To locate an appropriate counselor, I suggest that you "shop around" the way one might shop for a new car. Make out a list of what you want in a therapist. I mean this literally. Sit down and write out what you need someone to provide for you. Here are a few items that may help:

1. LOOK FOR A PROFESSIONALLY TRAINED PSYCHOTHERAPIST OR SPIRITUAL DIRECTOR WITH WHOM YOU HAVE NO PERSONAL OR PROFESSIONAL RELATIONSHIP.

It is important to locate a counselor with whom you can freely explore your inner world and re-examine how you will interact with others in your outer world. It is difficult for a Messiah to reveal vulnerabilities in the most conducive circumstances. An additional barrier to honesty is constructed by selecting someone who may be a friend of the family, a member of the congregation, a professional colleague or who may be dependent on you in some way.

It is critical that you locate a counselor with whom you can be honest without jeopardizing your professional or personal life. Since so many Messiahs are involved in the helping professions, it may be quite difficult to locate another minister, therapist, or spiritual director with whom you do not have a pre-existing or dual relationship. In some cases, the counselor may not be previously known to you but you may find that you have significant relationships in common—perhaps he or she went to school with a close friend, teaches the Sunday School class your four year old attends, or sits on the agency board for whom you work. Professional circles are often tightly knit, and locating an appropriate counselor may take some effort. Some Messiahs are well-known teachers, writers, ministers, or entertainers. Your notoriety may complicate the process of finding someone who will allow you to be who you really are. It may even be necessary to drive to another city. The most effective relationship between you and your counselor will be one that is free of competing roles and overlapping expectations.

2. SEEK PROFESSIONAL EXPERTISE THAT GENERATES A FEELING OF TRUST.

In order to build a level of trust in your counselor to the point where you may be willing to relinquish the Messiah role, you will need to feel that your counselor's professionalism is, at the very least, on a par with your own. Most Messiahs believe that they are the best, the smartest, and the most insightful. It is critical to select a counselor that generates a feeling of confidence and security.

Feel free to "interview" therapists as you would interview prospective employees. Ask them about their training, their licensing, and their philosophy of therapy. If they use terms with which you are unfamiliar, ask them to explain. If you feel confused by the jargon or feel foolish for asking, such feelings may indicate that this counselor is not for you. You are looking for someone who is secure in him or herself and his or her training, someone who is not trying to earn a sense of worth via the counseling role. A therapist who cannot handle an interview may also be unable to deal with feelings you may need to explore in future sessions. If you do not experience a sense of security and clear communication, feel free to cross that therapist off your list.

3. SEEK A COMPATIBLE WORLD VIEW.

This category is important for every Messiah. For two people to work together on inner regions of the psyche and spirit, they must share basic concepts about how the world works. It is important, in selecting a therapist and certainly a spiritual director, to be clear about the parameters with which you are comfortable. What are your spiritual beliefs? How do you view your role in life? Feel free to discuss your beliefs and concerns. If such matters are difficult to discuss in the session, once again, this counselor may not be the one for you.

4. FIND SOMEONE WHO IS NOT A "PRACTICING" MESSIAH.

Determining whether a counselor is a practicing Messiah is difficult, as it is very unlikely that you will be able to ask, "So, are you a Messiah?" For the answer to this question, you may have to rely on clues. Is the counselor rushing from appointment to appointment, obviously overextended? That may be because the counselor is caught in the Messiah Trap and has difficulty saying "no". Does the counselor hold you responsible for your own behavior or tend to take responsibility for (and control of) your growth? Is the counselor overly accommodating? Overly rigid? Look for such clues during your interview.

5. TAKE CARE OF YOUR ADDITIONAL CONCERNS.

You may have additional concerns and special issues. Feel free to take the time to examine your needs and express them in the interview.

6. PICK THE BEST COUNSELOR FOR YOU.

Often people take the first counselor they meet because they somehow feel obligated to do so. And it is certainly a typical Messiah response to feel that one "should" continue with a particular therapist in order to protect his or her feelings. The Messiah, caught in yet another angle of the Messiah Trap, may pay for counseling that is not helpful. As you look for a counselor, please feel free to be picky. After all, you are worth it.

SUPPORT GROUPS

Support and self-help groups have long proven themselves valuable arenas for facilitating healing. Self-help groups bring together peers, people who struggle with similar problems and together support one another through the journey of growth. Alcoholics Anonymous, for example, has a long history of success in helping people addicted to alcohol. Other groups in its model have been established to aid people suffering from a wide variety of addictions such as eating disorders, child abuse, and sexual dysfunction. Since Messiah behavior has an addictive component to it, people caught in the Trap can be greatly helped by the AA approach.

As a recovering Messiah, you need to experience the fact that you are just as broken as anyone else, just as valuable as anyone else, and your healing is just as possible as anyone else's. One way to experience this reality is by participating in a support group.

When involved in a Messiah support group, it is important to be aware of the special traps into which Messiahs tend to fall. A Messiah support group has inherent problems in that it is a gathering together of peers, all of whom are uncomfortable with and unskilled at interacting on a peer level. Messiah participants are highly skilled, however, at taking on roles of leadership. Consequently, each Messiah will tend to jockey for the role of leader. This competition may be subtle or obvious. Group members will need to continually look out for this dynamic and to draw attention to it whenever it occurs.

In order to illustrate the particular approach each Messiah style tends to use in gaining control and sidestepping intimacy, I will describe a hypothetical "Messiahs Anonymous" group, attended by examples of the seven Messiah styles:

Pleaser	Elizabeth	High school principal
Giver	Alicia	Single parent/Preschool teacher
Teacher	Gary	Professor/public speaker
Counselor	Diedre	Therapist
Crusader	James	Administrator
Rescuer	Dale	Attorney
Protector	Paul	Pastor

Picture, if you will, a living room filled with comfortable chairs, a couch, and floor pillows. In front of the couch is a coffee table. People are milling around in random fashion, uncertain where to sit.

Elizabeth: (looking at her watch) Well, it's a little after 7 P.M. but not everyone's here yet.

Alicia: (enters with a plate of cookies, which she places on the coffee table) I thought I'd bring these along for us to munch on while we talk.

Gary: Great. The only way Elizabeth could talk me into coming to this thing was to promise me you'd be here with your famous chocolate chip cookies.

Alicia: I've got more in the car if we run out. After the meeting tonight, I'm dropping some cookies and groceries by Mrs. Alvers's house. She's been ill. I'm hoping to save some cookies for tomorrow, though. My kids are having a party at school that I volunteered to coordinate.

Elizabeth: (looking again at her watch) Well, it's about ten minutes after 7. Everyone is here but Dale. I think we should go ahead and get started anyway. Just sit wherever you'd like.

The participants sit around the room. There is an awkward silence while everyone looks to Elizabeth for instructions.

Elizabeth: Well, I'll start off but I don't want to end up being the leader since the goal of this group is peer support. I've invited you here because I realized I need the support and a place where I can talk things out. What are some of the things you are expecting from this group?

Gary: I expect Alicia to bring something good to eat each week. (Group members laugh.)

Diedre: In the groups I lead in my practice, we set rules for confidentiality. I want to feel that what I may say here will go no further.

James: I agree with that. What I want to know is what we intend to accomplish. I've got too much to do to just sit around and shoot the breeze.

Diedre: What sort of things would you like to accomplish?

James: I don't know exactly. I am feeling rather agitated now, like I should be stuffing envelopes or folding fliers. I'm not used to sitting around doing nothing.

There is a knock on the door and Dale dashes in.

Dale: I'm so sorry to be late. What a day! One crisis after another. (heads straight for the phone) I'll be right with you but I've got to call my answering service and let them know where I am. With the way things have been going, they may need to get hold of me tonight.

The group waits until Dale returns.

Dale: I really should get a beeper.

Gary: Dale, we have been talking about what we expect out of this group. So far Diedre has tried to get us to take a vow of secrecy and James is trying to get us to launch a letter-writing campaign.

Paul: (smiling) As usual, Gary exaggerates.

Gary: Why do you think I draw such crowds when I speak? Because I'm boring? So, what do you want out of this group, Dale?

Dale: Well, I need a place where I can feel supported, a place where I can talk out some of my doubts. I can't do that at work. They depend on me to have the answers there.

Alicia: It seems like everyone in my life depends on me, too. I just can't be there for everyone like I'd like to. Several of my friends have been offended when I said I couldn't cook something for a potluck or contribute to a baby shower gift.

Diedre:	How did you feel about that?
Alicia:	(tears start to well up in Alicia's eyes) I am giving everything I can. It hurts to let them down but also makes me angry to think that the only thing that keeps my so-called friends in my life is my giving. Once I need some space, everyone gets huffy and disappears.
Diedre:	Did you express these feelings?
Alicia:	(hesitates) How did I get on the hot seat here?
Paul:	Diedre's just trying to help. Perhaps we should change the subject.
Diedre:	I'm sorry, Alicia. I didn't mean to make you feel uncomfortable.
Paul:	The most important thing to me is that we be sensitive to each others' feelings. I don't want to get involved in some intense group where we upset each other.
Dale:	(patting Alicia on the shoulder) Are you OK?
Alicia:	(pulling away) Sure, I'm OK.

The phone rings. Elizabeth answers it.

Elizabeth:	Dale, it's for you.

Dale goes to the phone, talks briefly, and puts on his coat.

Dale	Sorry, but an emergency just came up and I've got to leave.
Elizabeth:	Before he goes, let's decide what time we'll meet next week.
Gary:	This is a good time for me. How about the rest of you? (The group agrees.)
Elizabeth:	OK, same time next week. And please, let's try to start on time.

From this portion of group discussion, the various Messiah styles begin to reveal themselves:

Elizabeth, the Pleaser, concerns herself primarily with the structure of the group—the time, the location, the seating. She has difficulty participating in the discussion, however, once the topic focuses on feelings. Elizabeth withdraws once she launched the session.

Alicia, the Giver, brings her "Messiah" offering of cookies and receives the hoped-for reward through Gary's attention. Alicia tries to express her feelings but becomes very uncomfortable when she begins to display genuine feelings by way of her tears.

Gary, the Teacher, subtly picks up the role of leader through his humor and by directing questions to the other participants. He is careful to speak often but not to express his feelings in any depth.

Diedre, the Counselor, competes with Gary for the role of group leader. Like Gary, she tends to ask other participants questions. Diedre's questions, however, are more pointed and feeling-oriented than are Gary's. Her one comment about confidentiality comes more from her professional style of beginning groups in her practice, rather than expresses her own needs for safety. Diedre has no intention, at least at the time of this first meeting, to reveal anything about herself that would warrant confidentiality.

James, the Crusader, feels the urge to turn the support group into a task-oriented group. He has a need to "accomplish" something, which for him means to produce a tangible product. Groups in which James feels most comfortable are those with printed agendas and filled with activities. The discussion of feelings result in nothing tangible, and so James experiences anxiety about doing "nothing."

Paul, the Protector, sees Alicia as being in danger as she exposes her feelings to the group. Paul jumps into the discussion on Alicia's behalf, trying to mediate between Alicia and Diedre. His comment about desiring a safe group is intended to serve as protection for Alicia. He is still unaware of his own needs for safety, as he is ignoring his feelings and focusing solely on Alicia's.

Dale, the Rescuer, rushes in late and leaves early as he flies from crisis to crisis. He has nothing to say unless it involves a crisis and contributes only when he suspects that Alicia is troubled, to the point of emotional crisis. His attempt to put her in such a needy role fails as Alicia pulls herself together and resumes a staunch Messiah stance.

This example of a Messiah support group can give some insight into ways such groups can be helpful. Messiah participants can become more aware of the ways various styles are acted out. It may happen that some of the group members, those who are more willing to share their fears, will be branded as needy and those who are more willing to share their failures will be looked down with disapproval. Healing will come, however, as these Messiah Styles are discarded and participants relate to one another as equals. When members hide behind a caregiver role (and believe me, they will), it is important for the group to point this out and deal with it as a group.

Since some groups may be "taken over" by an especially aggressive Messiah, it may be helpful to bring in an official moderator who will take on a formal leadership role. This will provide the group with role clarity, which may be needed by participating Messiahs. The presense of a skilled group facilitator may allow the members to feel free to relinquish their sense of responsibility for other group members and to feel safe enough to focus on their own needs.

In addition to participating in a group which is designed to address the Messiah Trap directly, it may also be helpful to belong to support groups which facilitate personal growth in general—just as long as you are not the leader. As a participant, you may benefit from joining parenting support groups, prayer groups, marriage encounter groups, and so on. The most helpful groups will be those which focus on the expression of feelings among peers, and the least helpful will be those which focus on acquiring "information" or allow members to hide behind intellectual debate.

Appendix B: The Victim-Offender-Messiah Response Pattern to the Victimization Experience

This section presents the theoretical framework on which I based the book *When Helping You is Hurting Me.* The issues described in the book deal primarily with the role of the Messiah. In contrast to the book, this model addresses the coping strategies people may develop when they are victimized, and the role of the Messiah is but one of three that may develop in response to the experience of victimization. These roles are the Victim, the Offender, and the Messiah.

While any reader may benefit from an understanding of the theoretical framework, this section is primarily aimed at mental health professionals who may be treating clients participating in one of these three roles. This model, which I call the Victim-Offender-Messiah (V-O-M) Response Pattern, will be described in the following sequence:

1. V-O-M Response Pattern—Summary Statement
2. Parameters of the V-O-M Response Pattern Model
3. Trends in the Literature
4. The Victim-Offender-Messiah Response Pattern
5. Comparison of the V-O-M Triad
6. Issues in Treatment
7. Issues for the Therapist
8. Need for Future Study and Research

1. V-O-M RESPONSE PATTERN—SUMMARY STATEMENT

The Victim-Offender-Messiah Response Pattern is a theoretical model based on clinical observation and current trends in the literature. It may aid in treatment and prevention of child abuse and as a focus for future study and research. Although children's responses to various victimizing experiences are varied and complex, some people victimized as children may cope by participating in the V-O-M Response Pattern.

The V-O-M Response Pattern describes three roles around which people victimized as children may unconsciously build their identities and relationships:

1. The Victim internalizes the victimization experience by perceiving and promoting himself or herself as powerless and deserving of mistreatment.
2. The Offender attempts to reject the victimization experience by perceiving and promoting himself or herself as powerful and entitled to violate the boundaries of others.
3. The Messiah attempts to reject the victimization experience by perceiving and promoting himself or herself as a caregiver or protector of Victims and as a controlling agent of Offenders.

All three roles of the V-O-M Response Pattern are dysfunctional coping styles because the childhood victimization experience is not adequately addressed and resolved by any of the three players. The Victim unconsciously embraces the victimization experience, while the Offender and the Messiah unconsciously deny their victimization experiences. Their unresolved childhood trauma becomes a focal point around which the Victim, Offender, and Messiah unconsciously structure their identities and relationships. Therapy consists of helping clients develop alternative coping strategies that directly address the victimization experience. Clients may then be encouraged to develop an identity with relationship patterns based upon a nonvictimization point of reference.

2. PARAMETERS OF THE V-O-M RESPONSE PATTERN MODEL

In order to apply the V-O-M Response Pattern usefully it is important to understand its limitations. The V-O-M Response Pattern is not intended to be a fully comprehensive explanation of how people respond to victimization. No model can explain reality or even a particular phenomenon in its entirety. Our complex world provides us with the task of developing a variety of models and theories that can be used singly or in concert when they prove beneficial and modified or discarded when they are inadequate. The V-O-M Response Pattern was developed to bridge a gap in current theoretical frameworks addressing the response to victimization and is most useful when applied in conjunction with other compatible frameworks.

Though the V-O-M Response Pattern addresses the role of Offender, this model is not intended to address the complex forces that help create Offender behavior. This distinction is crucial. The V-O-M Response Pattern describes three roles a person may develop in response to childhood victimization. One of these responses may be to take on the Offender role. The reverse, however, is not necessarily true. While many adults who abuse and assault others were victimized as children, this model does not promote the idea that all Offenders were victims of childhood trauma.

The literature and direct experience drawn on in order to develop this model come primarily from the field of child sexual abuse. Consequently, the V-O-M Response Pattern reflects the idiosyncracies of those populations affected by child sexual abuse. As a result, the V-O-M Response Pattern may be more applicable to some victim populations that to others. Certainly the application of this model to any victim population must be done carefully and thoughtfully.

It is also important to clarify the terms used in this model. In the "Trends in the Literature" section of this Appendix, terms such as "child sexual abuse victim," "sex offender," and "child molester" refer specifically to people who have been victimized or who have perpetrated child sexual abuse. In the V-O-M Response Pattern, the terms "Victim," "Offender," and "Messiah," do not refer to specific individuals involved with child sexual abuse. Rather these terms delineate roles that people may take on in response to victimization. The "victimization experience" is not limited to child sexual abuse but includes any type of situation that disrupts normal childhood development. The "Victim" is not merely someone who has been traumatized, but a *role* one takes on with an identity and relationship pattern based on powerlessness and a feeling that the victimization was deserved. The term "Offender" is not limited to those who have perpetrated child sexual abuse but refers to a *role* with an identity and relationship pattern based on a sense of entitlement to any type of behavior including that which violates the boundaries of others. The term "Messiah" is reserved for the "super-helper," a *role* encompassing identity and relationship patterns based on an exaggerated sense of responsibility for the care of others.

3. TRENDS IN THE LITERATURE

In recent years American society has "discovered" the problem of child abuse. More specifically, it has acknowledged child sexual abuse. The literature has focused increasingly on the impact that childhood sexual victimization may have on the victim's subsequent functioning. Initially, research subjects were grouped as either victims or offenders.

Numerous studies have brought attention to the severity of the problem by identifying the prevalence of child abuse and its negative impact on the victim (Landis, 1956; Finkelhor, 1978; Finkelhor, 1979; Russell, 1983; Finkelhor and Hotaling, 1984; Brown and Finkelhor, 1984). The response to childhood victimization varies with each child and appears to be influenced by a variety of factors, which may include the age of the victim at the time of the molestation, the duration of the molestation, the level of violence and physical trauma experienced by the victim, the responses of others when the molestation was disclosed, and the relationship between the victim and offender (MacFarlane, 1978; Gelinas, 1983). There is indication that the traumatizing impact increases when the victim and the offender have close emotional ties (Sgroi, 1975).

During the sexual abuse episode, the child is physically and/or emotionally overpowered by the offender and coerced into sexual activity. Some children respond to the experience of victimization by internalizing an identity that revolves around helplessness and violated vulnerability. As MacFarlane (1978) observes

Most children are unprepared and unable to protect themselves against what is perceived as adult prerogative. As a result, many of them internalize their roles as victims within the sexual relationship and in the broader context of their own worlds. It is the instilling of this 'victim mentality' in the mind and the developing personality of a young girl [child victim] that is, perhaps, the most insidious aspect of her sexual exploitation. It is not only pervasive in the many areas of her life in which it may be reenacted, it is an extremely difficult self-concept to change and can be a devastating source of continued self-depreciation.

Paralleling victim-focused research, a variety of studies have addressed the perpetrators of these crimes (Gebhard, Gagnon, Pomeroy, and Christenson, 1965; Groth, 1978; Groth, 1979, and Groth and Hobson, 1983). Offenders as a group, were initially perceived as separate from the victim population, probably because of the generally held bias that offenders tended to be male while victims tended to be female. While most initial models developed to explain offender behavior may have included childhood dynamics or trauma, incidents of childhood sexual trauma in the lives of offenders were rarely cited (Shorr, 1965).

Not until fairly recently have sexual abuse victims and sex offenders been viewed as often sharing a common experience—that of childhood physical and/or sexual violation (Longo and McFadin, 1981; Groth, 1979). Groth states that the majority of the child molesters with whom he has worked were themselves victims of child sexual abuse. He postulates that, as children, these young male victims attempted to overcome their childhood trauma by reversing the roles and acting as offenders rather than victims (Groth, Hobson and Gary, 1982).

The conceptual division between victims and offenders has further blurred as research has begun to focus on the population of female offenders (Finkelhor, 1984). While samples are small, initial studies indicate that child sexual abuse is indeed a crime perpetrated by adult females. Some experts suggest this may occur at a higher rate than was previously anticipated. As may be expected, adult female offenders tend to have a history of sexual victimization in their childhoods. Furthermore, the types of offenses perpetrated by adult females seem to be influenced by the relationship that existed between the offender and herself as child victim (McCarty, 1986).

Innovative treatment programs are beginning to identify sexually abused children, some as young as three years of age, who are sexually abusing other small, more helpless children. The combined observations strongly suggest that children of either gender may respond to the victimization experience by developing an identity, behavioral repertoire, and a pattern for relationships based on an offender role.

Research and clinical literature addressing itself to incest has suggested a third response to the victimization experience. Some children, often female incest victims, respond to victimization by developing a caretaker role. The process of "parentification," by which a victim takes on a caretaker role is described by D. Gelinas (1983).

In parentification a child comes to function as a parent; she gradually does the cooking and laundry, provides the finances, provides the child care or in other ways takes care of the parents. Through gradual and usually unwitting induction by her parents, she begins not only to perform task functions but to assume responsibility for these functions ./. . She begins to form her self-identity around the notion that she has responsibility for caring for people, but they have no responsibility to care for her in return. Essentially she has no rights to reciprocity. In time she may no longer realize that she has legitimate needs of her own.

There is a gap in the literature regarding the prevalence of adopting the caregiver role and the relationship patterns common to someone in this role. In response to this need, the following description is presented to serve as a beginning point for future discussion, study, and research.

4. THE VICTIM-OFFENDER-MESSIAH RESPONSE PATTERN

Children raised in nonvictimizing environments are allowed to proceed through the natural stages of development. Parents make this process possible by maintaining proper role boundaries that allow children to confront life's tasks at an age-appropriate pace. When raised in an atmosphere of safety, these children move into adulthood with an identity based on a realistic sense of power and responsibility and an internalized sense of worth. Nonvictimized individuals are more likely to see the relationship between their actions and resulting consequences and to take responsibility for their choices.

By contrast, a victimizing experience disrupts the child's natural development. When adults violate or fail to protect children, the children's sense of power is damaged. These children are forced to prematurely take on the task of self-protection and often blamed for the abuse. Consequently, victimized children may experience a loss of power but an increased sense of responsibility. Combined with the degradation that often accompanies emotional, physical, and sexual violation, the child's self-esteem is often undermined. The identities often developed by victims of abuse are therefore based on a skewed sense of power, responsibility, and low self-esteem.

The response children have to victimization is varied. Three of the responses they may unconsciously choose are the Victim, the Offender, and the Messiah. Each of these roles struggle with a aviolated sense of power, responsibility, and self-esteem. The following describes how these three roles address these issues (See Chart F for comparison of V-O-M triad).

THE VICTIM

Rather than label the abusive behavior as the responsibility of the assailant, child victims often conclude that they were victimized because there was something in them that attracted such treatment. When a victim of abuse uses some defect in him or her to explain the abuse, that victim takes on the role of Victim. On an unconscious level, the Victim says, "I am treated poorly because I deserve this. I am victimized because I am a Victim." Victims relinquish power over their well-being but nevertheless feel responsible and "to blame."

VICTIM (Chart A)

Initial response to victimization:	Embraces victimization
Sense of power:	Releases control
Sense of responsibility:	Feels "to blame"
Self-esteem:	Low

Victims tend to recreate their early childhood victimizing experiences in the relationships they establish as older children and as adults. For example, Victims may select abusive marital partners and allow themselves and their children to suffer abuse. In this way Victims unconsciously help perpetuate the victimizing situation. It is important to clarify that I do not consider the victims of abuse to be responsible for their trauma. That responsibility falls solely on the shoulders of their assailants. People who develop identities as Victims, however, do not exercise the self-protective power they actually have and participate in ongoing abusive relationships and situations. Victims contribute to the perpetuation of abuse to the extent that they consciously or unconsciously subject themselves to ongoing victimization. They appear to be "addicted" to crises and to victimizing relationships.

THE OFFENDER

A second response that may be made by the abuse victim is that of taking on the role of Offender. The Offender is the individual unconsciously struggling to reject the notion that the victimization resulted from his or her own inferiority. This struggle has merit in that the Offender tries to claim. "I do not deserve this treatment. I am not a Victim." Rather than deal with the victimizing experience directly, however, the Offender tends to deny the occurance or impact of any such hurtful events and subsequent feelings of helplessness. While the attempt to hold onto self-esteem may be seen as positive, the Offender chooses to identify with the powerful role of assailant. Someone in this role relinquishes responsibility over his or her behavior and attempts to exercise power over others.

OFFENDER (Chart B)

Initial response to victimization:	Denial of victimization
Sense of power:	Takes control
Sense of responsibility:	Feels entitled but will not take responsibility for own behavior
Self-esteem:	Low

Though denying the victimization experience, the Offender is affected nevertheless. Driven to resolve this inner pain, Offenders seem compelled to reconnect with their childhood trauma. Consequently, Offenders try to recreate their victimizing situation by abusing someone who may reflect their childhood vulnerability. Apparently the act of victimizing another person serves to temporarily equalize the inner tension. Offenders experience a sense of satisfaction in perpetrating abuse because they project their own victimization onto another human being and force the victim to bear the pain that theythemselves refuse to feel. Their need to victimize others can become an addiction.

Some Offenders abuse others in similar ways they themselves were abused, suggesting that this "mirror" behavior may result from learned relationship patterns. Offenders, in order to re-create their childhood, seek out and establish relationships with Victims.

THE MESSIAH

The choice of the term "Messiah" may warrant explanation. While "Victim" and "Offender" are terms commonly used by professionals in the area of child sexual abuse, the term "Messiah" is usually considered to be religious or theological. I chose "Messiah" because its unique combination of characteristics best reflect the components of this role. Culturally the term messiah refers to a divine messenger from God. To some, the messiah *is* God. At the same time, the messiah is one who cares and suffers for others and is eventually sacrificed and martyred while in service of others. I have deliberately distorted the term "Messiah" in order to describe anyone, regardless of theological beliefs, with an exaggerated sense of responsibility and power to the point of grandiosity. Messiahs also suffer from low self-esteem and allow themselves to be sacrificed in what appears to be the care of others.

The Messiah, like the Offender, struggles to deny the occurance and negative impact of the victimization experience. The Messiah insists, "I am not a Victim," while at the same time unconsciously taking responsibility for the denied violation. Needing to regain a sense of power and control, yet unwilling to take on the Offender role, the Messiah unconsciously chooses the most powerful role available, that of helper. This approach, however, does not succeed in shielding the Messiah from the negative impact of the trauma. The Messiah develops an unrealistic sense of responsibility and low self-esteem.

MESSIAH (Chart C)

Initial response to victimization:	Denial of victimization
Sense of power:	Takes control
Sense of responsibility:	Grandiosity
Self-esteem:	Low

Unlike Offenders, Messiahs do not attempt to "create" Victims. Messiahs instead try to "save" Victims. Driven by the same unconscious needs experienced by Offenders, Messiahs externalize their pain by trying to help those who have been hurt in ways reminiscent of their own childhood victimization. There is a similar compulsive aspect to the Offender's need to hurt and the Messiah's need to heal. Both Messiahs and Offenders can become addicted to their relationships with Victims.

5. COMPARISON OF THE V-O-M TRIAD

ABILITY TO SET LIMITS

None of those in the three roles are able to set or protect appropriate relational boundaries. Victims cannot properly nurture themselves nor establish protective limits in relationship to others. Offenders tend to invade the emotional and physical space of others in a destructive, self-serving manner. It is common for Offenders to violate others and be oblivious to their harmful behavior. Messiahs also invade the emotional and physical space of others but do so under the guise of helping. Messiahs, like Offenders, are rarely aware of the harmful impact of their behavior.

Like Victims, Messiahs seldom set self-protective limits. Messiahs typically disregard their own needs, even to the point of denying that they have needs, and become overly involved in caring for others (See Chart F for comparison of the V-O-M triad).

POWER AND RESPONSIBILITY

Unable to set or honor proper boundaries, those in the three roles become enmeshed. They inappropriately distribute a sense of power and responsibility. Offenders assume they are entitled to take what they want from whomever they choose but are not to be held responsible for the consequences of their actions. As the Offender relinquishes proper responsibility, both the Messiah and the Victim take on this responsibility. Victims see themselves as the cause of the Offenders' abusive behavior. Messiahs attempt to contain the abuse perpetrated by Offenders.

V-O-M COMPARISON OF POWER AND RESPONSIBILITY
(Chart D)

	Power	*Responsibility*
Victim	Relinquishes control (−)	Takes responsibility (+)
Offender	Takes control (+)	Relinquishes responsibility (−)
Messiah	Takes control (+)	Takes responsibility (+)

Like the Offender, the Messiah is dependent on and addicted to a relationship with the Victim, who allows both to vicariously experience their inner disavowed pain. Both try in different ways to control the Victim. The Offender dominates the Victim through violation and coercion, while the Messiah maintains power over the Victim through a "helping" relationship. When controlled by Offenders, Victims often suffer more overt damage than when controlled by Messiahs. The Messiah nevertheless violates the boundaries of the Victim through "benevolent" control.

The Victim is victimized by both the Offender and Messiah, who hinder the Victim in exercising proper control over his or her life. In the original victimization experience, the Victim receives the message from the Offender, "You are inferior. You deserve this maltreatment." The Messiah revictimizes the Victim by conveying through the so-called helping relationship, "I agree with the Offender. You are inferior and you need me to protect you from the Offender." Neither the Offender nor the Messiah conveys a message of self-worth to the Victim.

CAPACITY TO EMPATHIZE

Empathy requires one to stretch beyond one's experience to understand and even experience the feelings of someone else. Victims tend to be self-focused and unable to feel anyone's pain but their own. Offenders are also self-focused but, because they deny the victimization experience, are unable to feel anyone's pain, especially that of Victims. Of the three roles, the Messiah would seem most likely to have the capacity for empathy, but they are no more able to genuinely empathize than are Victims or Offenders.

Messiahs use the pain of the Victim in an attempt to vicariously resolve childhood trauma. Consequently, Messiahs tend to feel only those feelings that originate from themselves. While they may appear to be empathizing, Messiahs are susceptible to projecting their own feelings onto Victims and are unable to view others as separate individuals with unique experiences and feelings.

INTERPLAY AMONG THE VICTIM-OFFENDER-MESSIAH TRIAD

Each member of the triad depends upon the other two to maintain equilibrium, though most often the triad breaks into dyads as the presence of all three players tends to overstress the balance of relationships. It is most common to find these players in teams of two, such as Victim-Offender, Victim-Messiah, or Offender-Messiah.

Each of the three roles are susceptible to addictive behavior patterns. Victims become addicted to crises and abusive situations and relationships. Offenders become addicted to creating victimizing situations and relationships. Similarly, Messiahs become addicted to crises, helping others, and relationships with Victims and Offenders.

I have presented the elements of the V-O-M Response Pattern as distinct categories, although in fact they often overlap. Since the Response Pattern provides three alternative coping styles, the victimized person may manifest all three by playing the Victim in some situations, the Offender in others, and the Messiah in still other arenas. Usually a person adopts one of the roles as a dominant identity, with the other two as complementary styles. An example of this dynamic is an adult client of mine who as a child was victimized sexually by her father. Even though she is now an adult, she continues to play the Victim role in her family system. As a professional in the mental health field, she uses the role of Messiah with her own clients, many of whom are victims of molestation. The Offender role manifests itself in her personal life, as she is emotionally cruel and exploitive with men.

6. ISSUES IN TREATMENT

Therapy must focus on helping the client develop alternative responses to the victimization process that allow him or her to directly confront and resolve the victimizing experience while at the same time avoiding merely moving the client from one point in the triad to another.

An example of how this role shifting happens emerges in the case of a young couple in which both the husband and the wife had been molested as children. The young man had been repeatedly assaulted sexually by several older boys when he was in grade school. In his early twenties, he married a young woman who, although it was unknown to him at the time, was a victim of incest. She was drawn to him "because he needed me," and the marriage was established on the basis of her playing the Messiah to his complementary Victim role.

In response to later marital tension, the couple entered therapy. The wife was the first to acknowledge her child sexual abuse, and a result of the attention to her victimization, their roles reversed and the wife became the Victim and the husband became the Messiah. She developed a profound sense of helplessness and fearfulness while he emerged as caregiver and protector. In the course of treatment, the wife became increasingly enraged over her childhood experience, an intense anger that she then aimed at her husband. She began to verbally and even physically abuse her husband, shifting the dyad once again. The Offender emerged, played by the wife, and the husband, taking his wife's abuse with a stance of helpless resignation, resumed his original role as Victim. It was at this point that he was willing to disclose his childhood victimization.

Unless the grip of this triad is broken, this couple could continue to alternate roles throughout their lives. It is also conceivable that therapists treating such couples may mistakenly conclude that the treatment is successful, since the clients seem to be addressing anger issues, disclosing victimization experiences, and opening communication. What may look like growth, however, is merely movement within the V-O-M Response Pattern. The clients are not genuinely growing.

The common issue among all Victims, Offenders, and Messiahs is the victimization experience. The pain of the childhood trauma must be unearthed and acknowledged and then redefined in such a way that the V-O-M Response Pattern may be discarded. In the first stage of acknowledging the victimization experience, the

Offender and the Messiah will offer the most resistance, as both have established their identities around the denial of their inner pain. These clients may need extensive experience with the therapist in order for enough trust to develop for them to withstand the stress of such self-disclosure. Until the Offender and the Messiah can confront their feelings of violation, however, they will remain entrapped in the V-O-M Response Pattern.

Once the victimization experience is achnowledged, Offenders and Messiahs must then gain a realistic understanding of power and responsibility. Clients are encouraged to relinquish responsibility for the abuse but to retain a sense of control over their lives. This is no simple task, as the therapist easily falls prey to setting up a dichotomy between the victim (this term refers, not to the role of Victim, but the the victim of abuse) and those who perpetrate abuse.

In the attempt to allow victims to release responsibility for their abuse, it is natural to place the "blame" for the abuse on the shoulders of the offender. It can be assumed, however, that all clients who have participated in the V-O-M Response Pattern have at one point or another taken on the Offender role. If the therapist sets up such a dichotomy, the client may feel free to acknowledge only those feelings and experiences that align with the role of Victim. The client may try to conceal any semblance of Offender behavior or impulses in an effort to avoid blame. By understanding the interplay between the three roles, the therapist can avoid this common error and instead encourage the client to take responsibility for choices that build self-esteem instead of falling into the trap of finding a "bad" person to blame.

As the therapist and Offender address issues of responsibility and power, it may be easy to assume that an Offender has progressed in treatment when he or she has actually taken on a Messiah role. I have observed treatment programs that have presented "model" Offenders to the public, those who are actively helping rather than perpetuating the problem. Though it is certainly preferable that we promote helpful rather than abusive behaviors, it is crucial to understand that these "new" Messiahs may return to their Offender behavior as long as they continue to participate in the V-O-M Response Pattern. An Offender must focus not on becoming a Messiah, but on establishing proper power and responsibility boundaries.

While Offenders must increase their sense of responsibility to include their own actions, Messiahs must place limits on their sense of grandiosity. Messiahs not only feel responsible for their own behavior but also for the choices made by Victims and Offenders. Messiahs often need encouragement to relinquish a sense of responsibility for everyone but themselves. They need permission to take care of their own needs and pain.

All three roles require assistance in common areas, such as the development of flexible and appropriate boundaries, the development of positive self-regard, and the establishment of relationships based on shared commonalities rather than the complementary, enmeshed roles of Victim-Offender-Messiah. Because of its addictive nature, all roles in V-O-M Response Pattern may benefit from individual therapy, group therapy, and self-help group support like that of Twelve-Step programs such as Alcoholics Anonymous and Al-Anon.

Alternative responses developed by the client may include the following characteristics (See Chart F for comparison with the V-O-M triad):

ALTERNATIVE (Chart E)

Initial response to victimization:	Acknowledgment of victimization
Sense of power:	Retains control
Sense of responsibility:	Feels responsible for own behavior only
Self-esteem:	Positive
Ability to set limits:	Can set limits on self, protects and nurtures self and others
Ability to empathize:	Self- and other-focused, is able to empathize without becoming enmeshed with others
Relationships with others:	Is capable of making relationships with peers, experiences own feelings independently of others

7. ISSUES FOR THE THERAPIST

In order to provide helpful treatment, the therapist must be aware of his or her own capacity to present clients with alternatives to the V-O-M Response Pattern. This entails an honest appreciation for one's propensity to participate in Messiah relationships with clients. Should the therapist establish a Messiah relationship with a client, whether the therapist be treating Victims or Offenders, the client's growth process will be stunted. While making the best of efforts to promote healing and growth in the lives of clients, a Messiah therapist unintentionally perpetuates the V-O-M Response Pattern.

In order for the therapist to help clients establish proper relationships, the therapist must first be able to participate in relationships that are not based on the V-O-M Response Pattern. Messiah mental health professionals exclusively relate to others according to the V-O-M triad and limit their relationships to include clients (Messiah-Victim or Messiah-Offender) or other Messiah therapists (Messiah-Messiah). They tend to develop workaholic lifestyles by becoming overinvested in their careers and overly involved with their clients. In addition, Messiah mental health professional tend to neglect their personal lives and the cultivation of peer relationships.

The delivery of effective therapy to others begins with the therapist's capacity to address countertransference issues as they relate to his or her own childhood experiences. The person whose needs come first in therapy are those of the client, not the therapist. However the therapist's own unacknowledged and unresolved victimization experiences may impair his or her ability to empathize with the uniqueness of each client's experience. Overidentification with the Victim's helplessness as well as a tendency to blame the Offender may result. To avoid using the client to meet unresolved victimization experiences, mental health professionals must be aware of their own inner needs, pains, and rages.

8. NEED FOR FUTURE STUDY AND RESEARCH

At present I have based the V-O-M Response Pattern on observation and experience, but further research is needed to test the accuracy of the model. Our mental health system responds more readily to Victims and Offender's leaving the needs of Messiahs unaddressed. Many individuals seriously traumatized by childhood victimization are not identified as needing help because they mask their pain through "helpful" Messiah behavior. As the saying goes, "the squeaky wheel gets the grease," and Messiahs don't tend to "squeak," but they are just as deserving and certainly as needy of understanding and treatment as are those identified as Victims and Offenders.

Studies are needed that address issues crucial to the V-O-M Response Pattern, such as those identifying specific family systems likely to promote the roles of Victim, Offender, and Messiah and intrapsychic response patterns to victimization. In addition, further exploration is needed into the role of mental health professionals and their susceptibility to taking on the Messiah role. Lastly a survey current therapeutic approaches and treatment programs to identify which may unintentionally encourage the V-O-M Response Pattern and which present genuine alternatives.

VICTIM-OFFENDER-MESSIAH RESPONSE PATTERN
(Chart F)

	Victim	*Offender*	*Messiah*	*Alternative*
Initial response to victimization	Embraces victimization	Denies victimization	Denies victimization	Acknowledges victimization
Sense of power	Releases control	Takes control	Takes control	Retains control
Sense of responsibility	Feels guilty, takes responsibility for Offender	Feels entitled, will not take responsibility for own behavior	Grandiose, takes responsibility for behavior of self, Victim, and Offender	Feels responsible for own behavior only
Self-esteem	Low	Low	Low	Positive
Ability to set limits	Cannot set limits, cannot protect or nurture self or others	Cannot set limits on self, invades others' space in destructive manner	Cannot set limits on self, invades others' space under guise of helping	Can set limits on self, protects and nurtures self and others
Ability to empathize	Self-focused, unable to empathize, unaware of needs of others	Self-focused, unable to empathize, unaware of needs of others, sees others as objects to meet own needs	Self-focused, unable to empathize, unaware of needs of others, over-identifies and enmeshes with others	Self- and other-focused, is able to empathize without becoming enmeshed with others
Relationships with others	Is incapable of developing relationships with peers, is violated by Offenders, depends on Messiahs for protection from Offenders	Is incapable of developing relationships with peers, depends on Victims, and looks to Messiahs to contain destructive behavior, uses Victims to experience own pain	Is incapable of developing relationships with peers, tries to protect Victims, and contains the destructive behavior of Offenders, uses Victims to experience own pain	Is capable of developing relationships with peers, experiences own feelings independently of others

References

Brown, Anela, and Finkelhor, David. 1984 (July). The impact of child sexual abuse—a review of the research. *Family Violence Research.*

Finkelhor, David. 1978 (September 11-15) Sexual victimization of children in a normal population. Paper presented to the Second International Congress of Child Abuse and Neglect, London.

Finkelhor, David. 1979. *Sexually Victimized Children.* New York: Free Press.

Finkelhor, David. 1984. *Child Sexual Abuse; New Theory and Research.* New York: Free Press.

Finkelhor, David, and Hotaling, Gerald. Sexual abuse in the national incident study on child abuse and neglect: an appraisal. *Child Abuse and Neglect,* 1984, 8:23–31.

Gebhard, P. H., Gagnon, J., Pomeroy, W., and Christenson, V. 1965. *Sex Offenders: An Analysis of Types.* New York: Harper & Row.

Gelinas, Denise. 1983 (November). The persisting negative effects of incest. *Psychiatry,* 46:312–32.

Groth, N. 1978. Guidelines for assessment and management of the offender. In *Sexual Assault of Children and Adolescents.* Lexington: Lexington Books.

Groth, N. 1979. *Men Who Rape: The Psychology of the Offender.* New York: Plenom.

Groth, N. 1979. Sexual trauma in the life histories of rapists and child molesters. *Victimology,* 4:10–16.

Groth, N., and Hobson, W. 1983. The dynamics of sexual assault. In *Sexual Dynamics of Anti-Social Behavior.* L. Schlesinger and E. Revitch, eds., Ill.: Thomas.

Groth, N., Hobson, W., and Gary, T. 1982. The child molester: Clinical observations. In *Social Work and Child Sexual Abuse.* New York: Haworth Press.

Landis, J. 1956. Experiences of 500 children with adult sexual deviants. *Psychiatric Quarterly Supplement,* 30:91–109.

Longo, Robert, and McFadin, Bradley. 1981 (December). *Law and Order* 29:21–23.

MacFarlane, Kee. 1978. Sexual abuse of children. In J. R. Chapman and M. Gates, eds., *The Victimization of Women.* Beverly Hills, CA: Sage. 3:81-109.

McCarty, Loretta. 1986 (September–October). Mother-child incest: Characteristics of the offender. *Child Welfare League of America,* 65:5.

Russell, Diana. 1983 (March). The incidence and prevalence of intrafamilial and extrafamilial sexual abuse of female children.

Sgroi, S. M. 1975. Sexual molestation of children. *Children Today,* 4:3.

Shorr, M., Speed, M. H., and Bartelt, C. 1965. Syndrome of the adolescent child molester. *American Journal of Psychiatry,* 22:783–789.

Further Reading

Beattie, Melody. *Codependent No More.* San Francisco: Harper/Hazelden, 1987.

Black, Claudia. *Repeat After Me.* Denver: M A C Printing and Publications, 1985.

Bolen, Jean. *Goddesses in Every Woman.* San Francisco: Harper & Row, 1984.

Fortune, Marie Marshall. *Keeping the Faith: Questions and Answers for the Abused Woman.* San Francisco: Harper & Row, 1987.

———. *Sexual Violence: the Unmentionable Sin.* New York: The Pilgrim Press, 1983.

Gallagher, Sister Vera with William F. Dodds. *Speaking Out, Fighting Back: Personal Experiences of Women Who Survived Childhood Sexual Abuse in the Home.* Seattle: Madrona Publishers, Inc., 1985.

Hawkins, Paula. *Children At Risk: My Fight Against Child Abuse—A Personal Story and Public Plea.* Maryland: Adler and Adler Publishers, Inc, 1986.

Johnson, Robert A. *He: Understanding Masculine Psychology.* New York: Harper & Row, 1977.

———. *Inner Work.* San Francisco: Harper & Row, 1986.

———. *She: Understanding Feminine Psychology.* New York: Harper & Row, 1977.

———. *We: Understanding the Psychology of Romantic Love.* San Francisco: Harper & Row, 1983.

Jung, Carl G. *Memories, Dreams, Reflections.* New York: Vintage Books, 1965.

Kelsey, Morton. *The Other Side of Silence: A Guide to Christian Meditation.* New York: Paulist Press, 1976.

Larsen, Earnie. *Stage II Recovery.* San Francisco: Harper & Row, 1987.

———. *Stage II Relationships.* San Francisco: Harper & Row, 1987.

Larsen, Earnie and Carol Larsen Hegarty. *Days of Healing, Days of Joy.* San Francisco: Harper/Hazelden, 1987.

Leonard, Linda S. *The Wounded Woman: Healing the Father-Daughter Relationship.* Boston: Shambhala, 1982.

McConnell, Patty. *A Workbook For Healing.* San Francisco: Harper & Row, 1987.

Maltz, Windy and Beverly Holman. *Incest and Sexuality: A Guide to Understanding and Healing.* Lexington: Lexington Books, 1987.

Miller, Alice. *The Drama of the Gifted Child.* New York: Basic Books, Inc., 1981.

———. *For Your Own Good.* New York: Farrer, Straus & Giroux, 1983.

————. *Thou Shalt Not Be Aware: Society's Betrayal of the Child.* New York: Farrar, Straus & Giroux, 1985.

Narramore, Kathy and Alice Hill. *Kindred Spirits.* Grand Rapids: Zondervan Publishing House, 1985.

Norwood, Robin. *Women Who Love Too Much.* Los Angeles: Jeremy P. Tarcher, Inc., 1985.

Parham, A. Phillip. *Letting God.* San Francisco: Harper & Row, 1987.

Peck, M. Scott. *The Road Less Traveled.* New York: Simon & Schuster, 1978.

Rachel V. *Family Secrets.* San Francisco: Harper & Row, 1987.

Rosellini, Gayle and Mark Worden. *Of Course You're Angry.* San Francisco: Harper/Hazelden, 1987.

Schaef, Anne Wilson and Diane Fassel. *The Addictive Organization.* San Francisco: Harper & Row, 1988.

Schaef, Anne Wilson. *Co-Dependence.* San Francisco: Harper & Row, 1987.

————. *When Society Becomes an Addict.* San Francisco: Harper & Row, 1987.

Schaeffer, Brenda. *Is It Love or Is It Addiction?* San Francisco: Harper/Hazelden, 1987.

Siegel, Bernie S. *Love, Medicine & Miracles.* New York: Harper & Row, 1987.

The Twelve Steps of Alcoholics Anonymous. San Francisco: Harper/Hazelden, 1987.